Lindsey,

Here's to

your

Success!

Praise for *Launch*

"*Launch* is your road map to success in an ever-changing world. Stelzner shows you how to enchant your customers so that they'll want to help you change the world."

—Guy Kawasaki,
author of *Enchantment*

"Hands on and generous, Michael shows you precisely how he does it, step by step."

—Seth Godin,
author of *Linchpin*

"If your business is flying high by making cold calls to sales prospects and by spending boatloads of money on ads, then you don't need the rocket fuel contained in this book. But if you're looking for a better way to reach the business heights you've only dreamed of, start reading *Launch*. Stelzner is a rocket scientist."

—David Meerman Scott,
author of *Real-Time Marketing & PR*

"What Stelzner shares here is proven! He's already built a community that propelled his brand not only beyond the competition but ahead of an entire industry. The stories he shares will help us do one of two things: excel or succeed."

—Brian Solis,
author of *Engage!*

"This isn't a book about marketing; it's about human nature. Understand that and you've unlocked the key to your success. Each chapter has a solid set of strategic and tactical recommendations for anyone in marketing. And the common theme throughout: *people*."

—Scott Monty,
head of social media
at Ford Motor Company

"I only believe what I've read in *Launch* because I've watched Michael Stelzner do it himself. It works."

—Chris Brogan,
president, HumanBusinessWorks.com
and co-author of *Trust Agents*

"Mike lays out—in a very easy-to-grok way—how to power your business's growth in a meaningful, measurable, sustainable way. Theory is fine, really. But what's even better is how-to action. And that's precisely what you'll find here."

—Ann Handley,
Chief Content Officer,
MarketingProfs and co-author of *Content Rules*

"Our company motto is 'Always Be Launching,' and it's served us well. Now, Mike Stelzner takes you behind the scenes of this powerful and effective online marketing strategy."

—Brian Clark,
CEO, Copyblogger Media

"I love books written by someone who has truly walked the path, and who shares the practical how-to steps for replicating his success, leaving nothing out. Mike Stelzner has done exactly that with *Launch*. He draws from his deep well of experience, spanning a decade launching two very successful businesses and quickly becoming a leading authority in both. Mike's teachings absolutely work! This book is a must-read for anyone serious about building a sustainable empire on a solid foundation in today's fast-moving, new media world."

—Mari Smith,
co-author of *Facebook Marketing:
An Hour A Day*

"The key paradox of modern marketing is that the more you 'sell' the less you sell. In *Launch*, Mike Stelzner has provided the perfect blueprint for this approach, demonstrating how to grow your business by being useful and solving problems. Mike's elevation principle alone is worth the purchase price. Buy this book and fuel your own meteoric rise."

—Jay Baer,
co-author of *The NOW Revolution*

LAUNCH

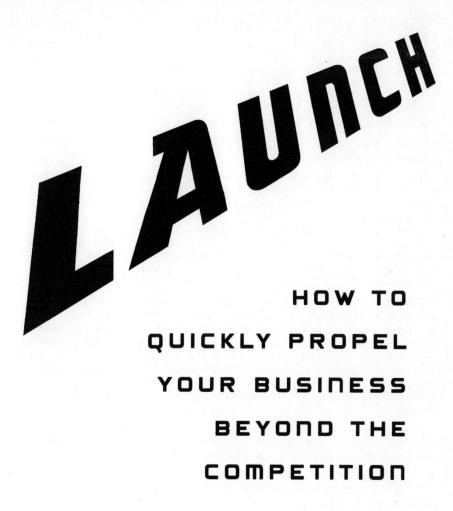

LAUNCH

HOW TO QUICKLY PROPEL YOUR BUSINESS BEYOND THE COMPETITION

MICHAEL A. STELZNER

WILEY

John Wiley & Sons, Inc.

Published by John Wiley & Sons, Inc., Hoboken, New Jersey.
Published simultaneously in Canada.

For general information on our other products and services or for technical support, please contact our Customer Care Department within the United States at (800) 762-2974, outside the United States at (317) 572-3993 or fax (317) 572-4002.

Wiley also publishes its books in a variety of electronic formats. Some content that appears in print may not be available in electronic books. For more information about Wiley products, visit our Web site at www.wiley.com.

Library of Congress Cataloging-in-Publication Data:

Stelzner, Michael A.
Launch: how to quickly propel your business beyond the competition/Michael Stelzner.
   p. cm.
Includes index.
ISBN 978-1-118-02723-3 (cloth)
ISBN 978-1-118-10276-3 (ebk)
ISBN 978-1-118-10277-0 (ebk)
ISBN 978-1-118-10278-7 (ebk)
  1. Marketing. 2. Marketing–Management.   3. Customer relations–Management.
  4. Business networks–Management.   5. Industrial promotion. I. Title.

HF5415.S755 2011
658.8–dc22   2011012873

Printed in the United States of America

10 9 8 7 6 5 4 3 2 1

For the person who's been told, "It can't be done," this is for you.

Contents

Preface

If you've ever been discouraged by the undelivered promises of marketing, this book is for you. You and I share something in common: We've hoped that our marketing efforts would bring us big results. We've tried and failed. We've dusted ourselves off and kept on trying—each time learning from our failures.

I wrote *Launch* for you. I've failed so many times I stopped counting. But along the way, I kept at it—relentlessly. Then, finally, things clicked.

My hope is that this book reveals a new way of marketing to you. It's one that involves focusing on the needs of others, giving gifts, working with outsiders, and caging your marketing messages. These principles are precisely the opposite of traditional marketing. Yet they work. And they are the future.

Let me give you a little preview of what's in store for your business.

I'd like you to think of your business as a rocket ship. Your goal is to navigate this powerful machine to new frontiers. Your fuel is great content.

People consume your fuel, moving your rocket higher and faster. Your marketing messages have been packed in long-term storage. As you travel to new galaxies, a huge community of your peers, prospects, and customers supports you. You've become unstoppable.

In older and smaller rocket ships are your competitors. They're stuck at the edge of the atmosphere. Gravity is not only working against them, many have crashed and are wondering what happened.

The world is changing. Now it's time for your business to change as well.

In this book you'll discover how to bring the masses to your business and become a hub for your marketplace—all without the need to constantly pitch your services or wares. The odds are no longer against you. Now you have a proven plan.

This book isn't like other marketing books. Rather than making keen observations about others who've achieved success, the ideas and principles in this book were developed, refined, and practiced by real businesses—my businesses. I'll reveal precisely how you can immediately implement the techniques found in this book. And of course I'll share how others have achieved success.

Here's how to use this book:

The ideal way to consume this book is to read it straight through. Study the first chapter. It'll reveal what's wrong with most marketing, and introduce you to the *elevation principle* (the main idea behind the entire book).

The second and third chapters are foundational. You'll learn how to put together a new mission plan for your business. You'll also discover how to set systems in place that ensure you never run out of ideas or inspiration.

Chapters 4 and 5 reveal the power of working with outside experts, how to find them, and how to recruit them. This is an essential part of the elevation principle that most businesses don't employ. Study this section carefully. It will be what sets you apart in your industry.

Chapters 6, 7, and 8 take you deep into the craft of creating engaging content—the fuel for your business. In these chapters I'll introduce you to *primary fuel* and *nuclear fuel*. Primary fuel is what keeps your business moving on a daily basis. Nuclear fuel is special content that moves your rocket ship very quickly and attracts the attention of many people.

Chapter 9 reveals what it means to cage marketing messages, and introduces you to new ways to employ marketing techniques. You'll discover that marketing doesn't need to be aggressive to achieve amazing results. Finally, in the Appendices, you'll find primary fuel content samples, to help you formulate your own.

Let today be the day you decide to set a new course for your business. It's my hope that this book will become your trusted guide. Study it. Employ the techniques. Watch what happens.

I've set up a companion site for the book at ElevationPrinciple .com. Be sure to stop by to watch free videos that provide more ideas to help you grow your business.

I'll see you out in space!

Acknowledgments

I'd like to start by acknowledging you for buying this book. Thanks! Here are some other people who deserve kudos.

First my family: Thanks to my wife and kids, for bearing with me during Thanksgiving and Christmas as I wrote this book! Thanks to my dad, for his feedback and encouragement. I'd also like to thank my Lord and Savior, Jesus, for providing me endless sources of inspiration. You rock!

To my team! I'd like to thank Phil Mershon, for providing critical analysis of every thought on every page of this book. Thanks to Cindy King, for her keen insight. Thanks to Court Patton of PattonBros.com, for the great illustration work in the book. And thanks to the fans of SocialMediaExaminer.com, who provided outstanding insight and support.

Also, thanks to Mike Volpe from HubSpot, and David Germano from Barefoot Proximity (managers of Man of the House), for giving me their inside scoops!

Finally I'd like to thank my friend David Meerman Scott, for encouraging me to get this book under way and for helping me make it happen. And thanks to Shannon Vargo at John Wiley & Sons, Inc., for believing in me!

Rockets Don't Fly Themselves

Everything in space obeys the laws of physics. If you know these laws, and obey them, space will treat you kindly.
—Wernher Von Braun, February 17, 1958

For businesses, change is guaranteed. Industries advance, ideas expand, products morph, and customers move on. Similar to space travel, everything's in orbit. Nothing remains still.

Whether you're just about to launch your rocket ship or you're already in flight, change is coming like a speedy comet. It won't bend to your will. You'll need to either embrace it or get out of its path.

Yes, it's scary. You and every other business owner, marketer, or budding entrepreneur have experienced the uncertainty of tomorrow. I've pondered these very thoughts: Will my business survive? Have I set the right trajectory? What's coming? Am I ready?

Despite the assurance of change, *there's something that remains fixed—and most businesses overlook it.* You've been watching for change and likely missed the one thing that has remained constant: people.

People don't really change. I'm talking about you, your customers, your partners, and your peers. They might leave you for a competitor, but at their core they haven't really changed at all. And people are what make or break your business.

1

People want valuable insight, access to great people, and recognition before *they want products and services.* If you can keep your eyes fixed on people and their desires, half your mission will be achieved before you begin.

My kids are girls. Have you ever tried brushing a moving child's hair? You either need to walk along with her or force her to stop. Too often, we treat our customers like children.

Stop trying to force customers to conform to your desires and instead walk beside them and see what happens.

People don't want to be pitched to, marketed to, or herded like cattle. People do want information, answers, access, and recognition—and they want it all for free.

Three Big Questions

1. *How can you attract leads, prospects, and opportunity without actively selling?* Imagine no cold-calling, no advertising, none of the kinds of activities that you either hate doing or you know costs a fortune.

2. *How can you gain access to influential people in your industry?* Is there an easy way to work with people who have the highest imaginable profile? If they were willing to help you, without hesitation, how would it impact your business?

3. *Is there an easy way to connect with and gain the trust of prospects and customers?* How can you cut through the noise and gain the attention of people? Is there a proven way to earn their trust and support?

The Problem with Marketing

I've been told marketing success means spending lots of money.

Here's how the American Marketing Association defines it: "Marketing is the activity, set of institutions, and processes for creating, communicating, delivering, and exchanging offerings that have value for customers, clients, partners, and society at large."[1] Yeah, it's a mouthful.

Focus on two words here: "exchanging offerings." Most of us have been taught that *marketing is about making an offer that attracts people.* We've been trained to focus on crafting the right arrangement of words and delivering them in the right place, at the right time, using the right medium.

We're treating people like fish. If we just create a better lure than our competitors, silently climb into a boat, and simply cast that bait right on top of our customers, they'll bite. Or so the theory goes.

And the word "exchange" implies a two-way process between the company and the customer. Your business makes an offer and the prospective customer is compelled to comply.

Frankly, if there weren't some level of truth to this, marketers would be out of business. I'll be the first to admit that I've successfully employed some of these very tactics.

But *here's where marketing lets us down*: It can't predict when people are ready to buy the type of widget you have to sell.

For example, I'm going to eventually need a new car. But right now I'm very happy with my existing car. There's no marketer out there who can predict with any degree of certainty when I'll be done with my car. Some might notice that I just incurred a huge repair bill. Others might make assumptions based on how long I've driven my car or how many miles I've accrued. But no one knows what will ultimately motivate me to ditch my car. Heck, I don't even know.

So marketers are forced to make educated guesses about me. Worse yet, they're forced to pay others to reach me.

To get in front of my eyes and ears, auto dealers and manufacturers must place ads in the magazines I read, sponsor commercials and placements during my favorite television shows, place ads on the Web sites I frequent, and get airtime while I'm in my car—just to mention a few.

At the time of this writing, the U.S. automotive industry was spending more than $400 to market each car sold, adding up to more than $4 billion annually![2]

---

[1] American Marketing Association. Definition of marketing (approved October 2007), www.marketingpower.com/AboutAMA/Pages/DefinitionofMarketing.aspx, 2010.

[2] "Nielsen: U.S. Ad Spending Up 4% in Q1," *Radio Ink* (October 2010), www.radioink .com/Article.asp?id=1982517&spid=30800.

Do you have that kind of money? Is your product or service profitable enough to include that kind of expense? Is your volume big enough to afford dropping millions of dollars into a campaign with no guarantees?

Is there a better way?

The Internet as the Great Paralyzer

The Web has changed business forever. It's the kind of change that has really scared established companies. And rightly so! Could this great equalizer also be the demise of businesses?

The idea of selling direct to consumers anywhere in the world has been transformative. It didn't just put travel agents, department stores, and newspapers out of business. It also allowed average Joes like us to compete. All of a sudden a good idea could gain traction and grow.

Businesses like Amazon and eBay became billion-dollar enterprises. Any information on any topic could be found instantly. And rich knowledge was available from anywhere—home, office, car, or the beach. Crazy ideas, like putting people's faces up on a Web site and enabling friends to connect, have brought people together by the hundreds of millions.

But for every Internet success story, there are a million ideas that never come to fruition. The success of the Web also prevents many people from taking action.

For example, back in the mid-1990s, I owned a creative services agency. We helped high-tech businesses look good. Our business was booming—until the day the tech market crashed. We lost a lot of business. I was faced with the ugly and unfamiliar face of change.

I decided to focus my business in a new area. I settled in on writing white papers (persuasive documents that help people make decisions). To my shock and horror, I discovered I was not the first agency to specialize in white papers. There were others.

My first reaction was, "Oh man, this sucks." And I pondered going back to the drawing board.

Maybe you know someone with a similar story?

Competing via the Web is a lot like graduating high school: You might have been the smart kid or the popular one at your school. But the second you headed off to college, you realized there were a lot more smart people. And maybe up against some of them, you were not so smart anymore.

The Internet takes local competition to a global stage. All of a sudden you're competing with hundreds or thousands of businesses. They're everywhere. Now you're up against smart folks from New Zealand, Germany, Russia, India, and Japan.

Stepping up to compete on a national or global stage can be very intimidating, and downright paralyzing. Maybe it's even been a hindrance to you?

How can you grow your business without massive financial investments? Is there an easy way to leverage the power of the Web without worrying about the competition?

Meet the Enemy: Channel Overload Syndrome

Is your attention fragmented? I know mine is!

Channel overload syndrome happens when information is transmitted faster than it can be received. It's like those intense rainstorms that cause raging rivers, taking out everything in their paths. Instead of pouring down rain, bucket-loads of information are dumping on the brains of your customers and prospects. And simple umbrellas don't cut it.

As a result, people are retreating, shutting down, and seeking refuge from the information onslaught. People are literally tuning out!

Think about it: Your e-mail inbox is crammed with a never-ending stream of messages, you have billions of possible Web sites to surf and videos to watch, your physical mailbox is full of junk mail, and everywhere you turn you see and hear commercials. Let's not overlook voicemails, text messages, instant messages, tweets, and Facebook updates. And what about those stacks of dusty magazines and unread newspapers?

All these choices present a huge problem for any business. If your customers aren't receiving your messages, they're likely not thinking about your business either.

So what can a business do? What are the obvious choices?

One option is to try to communicate across all the channels. Another choice is to ignore how the world is changing and do what you've always done.

If you attempt to engage all the channels, it will cost you a fortune, and you'll never be able to keep up. There are just too many, and new channels seem to be emerging each year.

Hiding your head under a pillow will also lead to your demise. If you can't see the need to change, you'll slowly shrink your audience and hinder your business.

Is there another option?

Do People Really Trust Your Business?

Fewer than one in three people trust marketing messages, according to Edelman Digital's annual survey of trust.[3] That's a pretty dismal number.

The study also found that *trusting companies is more important than delivering great products and services.*

Do your prospects and customers trust you?

If great products alone won't gain the trust of consumers, what will?

"For all companies, it's about laying foundations for sustainable growth by deepening relationships with customers, and, with trust in business arguably at an all-time low, that's not an opportunity that one should turn down lightly," said Jeremy Darroch, CEO of the U.K. broadcasting giant BSkyB.[4]

If the default position of customers and prospects is to distrust your business, successfully growing your business becomes a monumental challenge. "The strategic imperative for most companies is to do what they can to regain the trust of stakeholders and to more effectively manage relationships with them," stated a *Harvard Business Review* article.[5]

---

[3] Edelman Digital. 2010 Edelman Trust Barometer, www.edelman.com/trust/2010/docs/2010_Trust_Barometer_Executive_Summary.pdf.

[4] As cited in Hughes, M. "Business Must Help Us Restore Trust," *Evening Gazette,* November 8, 2010. www.nebusiness.co.uk/business-news/latest-business-news/2010/11/08/business-must-help-us-restore-trust-51140-27619359/.

[5] Beinhocker, E., Davis, I., & Mendonca, L. "The 10 Trends You Have to Watch," *Harvard Business Review* (July–August, 2009). hbr.org/hbr-main/resources/pdfs/comm/fmglobal/the-ten-trends-you-have-to-watch.pdf.

The Edelman report also found that people value guidance from credentialed experts significantly more than peers. This is one bright spot in an otherwise murky outlook for businesses.

Is there a way to establish your business as a trusted authority in your industry?

Introducing the Elevation Principle

Whether you're launching a new business, releasing a new product, or you need to transform your company, the elevation principle will quickly help improve your reputation, marketplace standing, and, yes, revenues.

I want to assure you that no matter what stage your business is at—from just getting under way to being grounded in decades of prior success—the techniques and tactics I reveal here will help transform your business. They'll prepare you for change. They'll help you grow.

The foundation for the elevation principle comes directly from the school of hard knocks (from which I graduated magna cum laude). I was never taught these concepts in graduate school. Rather, through 15 years of trial, error, tests, and failures, these principles were born and refined.

> Simply defined, the *elevation principle* is the process of meeting the core desires of prospects and customers by helping them solve their basic problems *at no cost*.

The elevation principle helps businesses gain the trust and attention of people by providing them highly desirable content that lacks any obvious marketing message or motive. Rather than ending every message with a blatant sales pitch, lighten up on the marketing messages.

The right content is highly sharable and can quickly draw important people to your business, enabling you to achieve rapid growth and soar beyond the competition, without the traditional costs of marketing.

START BY HELPING PEOPLE

Here's the premise: *If your marketing strategy centers on helping people with their smaller problems, many will seek your help to solve their bigger issues.* If you can multiply free assistance to hundreds, thousands, or millions of people, they'll help rapidly grow your business, elevating you beyond the competition, and enabling you to become an unstoppable industry force.

Why? Because *people's core desires don't change.* Everyone wants access to great insight and to knowledgeable people who can help them. You meet this desire by producing engaging and interesting content that meets people's insatiable demand for how-to information and assistance.

Your goal should be to trigger this thought in the minds of people: "If their content is this good, how much more valuable would their products or services be?" Triggering the "how much more?" question *is highly desirable* and will help turn lurkers into customers.

Whether you're selling consulting services, information products, events, expensive products, or low-cost commodities, you can use these techniques to break through the channel overload syndrome and establish lasting trust, all without traditional marketing efforts.

If you lift people up, they'll help lift you up.

Get Others Involved

Applying the elevation principle propels your business growth when *you shine the spotlight on people*, rather than focusing on yourself, your products, or your services. Those people should include successful peers outside your company, industry experts, and customers.

When you combine great content with great people, you quickly stand apart from others in your industry, attracting large numbers of prospective customers. Down the road, it will be those people who will propel your business beyond your competitors'.

Here are three quick examples of other-focused content efforts:

- ◆ If you offer consulting services, you could interview the author of a hot, new, and relevant book. This shares new insight with your readers and helps the author gain exposure. It could also lead to collaboration down the road between the author and your company.
- ◆ If you manufacture cooking products, you could showcase a popular chef's unique cooking tips. This provides to your base

useful ideas that might be implemented using your company's products, and helps the chef gain exposure to your audience.

◆ If you run a new private elementary school, you could showcase graduates from similar programs around the country. This helps prospective parents visualize what their children might achieve at your school. It also helps promote the graduates.

When you get other people involved with your content, you not only provide value to your audience, you also forge relationships that can result in long-term benefits to your business.

THE ELEVATION PRINCIPLE FORMULA

Here's the elevation principle in a simple formula:

$$GC + OP - MM = G$$

Spelled out, the formula reads: "Great Content" plus "Other People" minus "Marketing Messages" equals "Growth" (see Figure 1.1).

When you offer great content—such as detailed how-to articles, expert interviews, case studies, and videos—that focuses on helping other people solve their problems, you'll experience growth. The "other people" component transcends your reader base and involves reaching out to people outside your company, such as industry experts. All of this transpires in a marketing-free zone.

Once the marketing messages are caged, the focus of your company shifts from "What can we sell you?" to "How can we help you?" You shift from pitching products to boosting people. *Instead of investing in ad space, you invest in creating content, experiences, gathering points, and communities where people who need help can find it.*

You have the chance to *own* the place people go to for help, eliminating your reliance on traditional marketing channels. You can become the center of your industry, niche, or local market. And when that happens, you're launched on an unstoppable trajectory that will take you places you never imagined possible.

The result: You no longer need to sell! Instead, *you demonstrate your expertise by the content you produce, the ideas you showcase, the*

ELEVATION PRINCIPLE

FIGURE 1.1   The elevation principle says that great content plus other people minus marketing messages results in growth.

stories you share, and the people you attract. By creating a platform for others, you can also build strategic alliances, quickly grow a large following, and dominate your industry.

EXAMPLES

Here are two examples of the elevation principle in practice, one from an established $20-million business, and the other from a newer start-up.

HubSpot   HubSpot is an inbound marketing software company that helps small businesses generate leads and close sales.

Since its launch in 2006, HubSpot has grown to 200 employees, received $33 million in venture capital funding, and is on track to sell $20 million in services in 2011, a 350 percent growth from 2010.

What's unique about HubSpot is that its entire growth has been tied to content marketing efforts that focus on providing great value to others with few marketing messages.

"It's interesting that with a lot of these newer marketing techniques, you can really beat the big guys in a huge way, because they're usually tied to their older methods of doing marketing," said Mike Volpe, HubSpot's vice president of marketing.

Volpe, the company's fifth employee, has overseen the content marketing activities of HubSpot from the beginning. In the early years, the company had two primary content objectives: its blog and a special online tool called Website Grader (see WebsiteGrader.com).

Website Grader is a free tool that evaluates a Web site's marketing effectiveness by analyzing its content, search engine optimization, social media integration, and lead capture capabilities. The tool is very light on marketing messages and very heavy on valuable feedback, and has caught the attention of people like Guy Kawasaki, who promoted the product without solicitation.

More than 3 million people have evaluated their Web sites using Website Grader. It has also become one of the top two sources of quality leads for the company. "Once they've run a Website Grader report, they [prospects] become extremely interested in HubSpot," said Volpe.

HubSpot uses its blog as a powerful marketing tool. *Advertising Age* ranks the site as one of the top 25 marketing blogs on the planet. HubSpot's strategy is to publish multiple educational articles daily, with a focus on quality marketing-related content.

Webinars are also part of HubSpot's content marketing strategy. Each month, the company holds as many as 10 free webinars. One had 13,000 registrants. In addition, HubSpot has created 200 original videos and a weekly live Web TV show called "HubSpot TV," and regularly publishes ebooks.

"I think for the vast majority of companies, they add way too much of the marketing message in their content," said Volpe. "I think you need a little bit. But it's like a drop or two for every gallon of content. Most people try to cram as much of it in there as they can, and it totally devalues their content and makes it not interesting," he added.

HubSpot generates 25,000 leads per month for its 60-person sales team. One hundred percent of those leads come from its content marketing efforts.

Social Media Examiner   On October 12, 2009, I launched Social MediaExaminer.com. Our slogan was "Your Guide to the Social Media Jungle." The objective was to grow 10,000 e-mail subscribers before we sold anything. We were targeting business owners and marketers.

Prior to the launch of this site, my company had almost zero standing in the social media industry. It was mostly an unknown entity trying to compete in a quickly growing and already large marketplace—a market full of experts who were likely 10 times smarter than I was.

All the odds were against us.

On opening day, we held interactive live video broadcasts with four industry experts (see Figure 1.2).

We also recruited high-profile professionals to pen one article a month on our site. In the beginning, our goal was to publish three

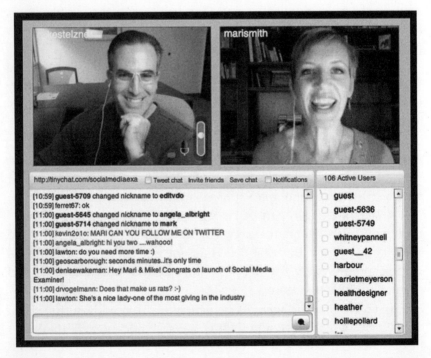

FIGURE 1.2   This is an example of a live video broadcast Social Media Examiner did on its opening day, with Facebook expert Mari Smith.

how-to articles each week that covered the hot topics of the time. We regularly interviewed industry gurus, and shared success stories from other businesses, revealing how they did what they did. Our goal was to provide other people's tips, ideas, and results to our readers. They loved it, and the professionals loved the exposure.

We didn't talk about what we were selling, and we didn't talk about ourselves at all. Instead, we identified the areas where our readers needed the most help and, simply, helped them. Our goal was to become a trusted resource by tapping the power of trusted resources.

Here were the results: Within 12 months, we went from zero to more than 40,000 e-mail subscribers, received 450,000 monthly page views, and acquired 20,000 Facebook fans. SocialMediaExaminer.com became one of the world's top 25 business blogs, according to *Advertising Age* and Technorati. Amazingly, according to Alexa, our site was also one of the top 1,700 Web sites in the United States.

In our niche, we became one of the world's top two social media blogs—nearly overnight. We also earned more than a million dollars in our first 12 months, directly attributed to our efforts—well beyond our little company's expectations.

■ ■ ■

These two success stories illustrate that when you elevate your message above the typical marketing hype and focus on helping people, you can achieve amazing results.

Elements of the Elevation Principle

The elevation principle combines great content and a focus on others while removing obvious marketing messages. *Think of content as the fuel for your rocket, and people as what ignites the fuel and directs the rocket.* Think of marketing as friction that slows your rocket's progress.

Here's an overview of the core components of the elevation principle:

GREAT CONTENT

Content comes in many forms. It's like highly refined rocket fuel that can take you places quickly.

Figure 1.3   Primary fuel is what keeps your business moving.

There are two different types of content. First there's ***primary fuel***: It's easy to produce and is what makes your business move.

Primary Fuel   You'll need the most of this type of content to achieve success. Without it, you'll have fits and false starts, likely sending your rocket ship in circles, or causing frequent stalls (see Figure 1.3).

There's a wide array of primary fuel available. Here's a brief overview of some of the options:

◆ *Comprehensive how-to articles:* Detailed in nature, this type of content is typically at least 1,000 words. It should show your readers how to do something they're interested in. For example, at SocialMediaExaminer.com, we target marketers. Mari Smith, one of our contributing writers, crafted a piece called "21 Creative Ways to Increase Your Facebook Fanbase." This type of content is typically widely shared, referenced, and commented on.

◆ *Expert interviews:* Every industry has its experts. These are the people who are frequently cited, speak at events, maintain popular blogs, or author books. Conducting interviews with these experts helps keep your audience informed of new trends and innovative ideas. Interviews can be in the form of video, audio recordings, or text-based articles. For an excellent example of video interviews, visit David Garland's TheRiseToThe Top.com site.

◆ *Reviews of books, products, and Web sites:* Most industries have experts who are regularly releasing books, new products, and online resources. By turning your readers onto good books, interesting noncompeting products, and useful sites, you become a valued asset for them. For example, WhitePaperSource .com puts out a monthly newsletter that often highlights studies showing the value of white papers for businesses. This type of content helps readers discover new ideas and resources.

◆ *Case studies:* Also known as *success stories,* case studies reveal people and/or businesses that are achieving success. The simple formula here involves revealing the challenges faced by a company, examining the action steps taken to overcome the challenges, and then showing the results. This type of content is very important because it showcases how others are achieving success, enabling readers to see how they might try similar tactics. An example from SocialMediaExaminer.com is "How Social Media Helped Cisco Shave $100,000+ Off a Product Launch," crafted by case study expert Casey Hibbard.

◆ *News stories:* If your industry is constantly breaking news, you could become the *source* that informs people of new products or services. The goal with this type of content is to quickly break a story before it goes mainstream. If you accomplish this, you can receive large spikes in traffic. For example, MacRumors.com does a great job of predicting what's coming next from Apple by scouring patent applications and leveraging informants.

◆ *Contrarian stories:* Examining the opposing view of a widely held idea can often be very effective. For example, I crafted an article for MarketingProfs.com entitled "The Dark Side of Twitter: What Businesses Need to Know," in February of 2009—at the peak of Twitter's frenzied growth. The article was the company's top-performing one for the year and brought enormous traffic to MarketingProfs.com.

Primary fuel can be used in many different places. Ideally, it's stored on a Web site under your control. It can also be distributed via e-mail, print, or video. If you don't have a large audience, primary content can be strategically published in places where your audience resides (like other people's blogs).

You can mix together different types of primary fuel or just focus on one type. For example, at SocialMediaExaminer.com we focus on how-to articles, expert interviews, and case studies.

Primary fuel provides the steady upward movement that your rocket ship needs. For quicker progress you'll need advanced fuel.

Nuclear Fuel   The most powerful type of business propellant is called *nuclear fuel*. This highly advanced superfuel is more difficult to produce. But if you have nuclear fuel, your rocket can achieve powerful boost, rapidly propelling you through different areas of space (see Figure 1.4). You'll do just fine using only primary fuel, but you won't move as fast or as far as you could.

You should, however, consider using nuclear fuel infrequently and only under carefully timed and executed strategies. When your business employs this type of content, you can move quickly, because it often attracts the attention of many people.

Most businesses never employ nuclear fuel. However, businesses that use this type of content often find themselves quickly standing out from their competitors.

There are fewer types of this fuel available. Here's a brief overview of some of the options:

◆ *Reports based on surveys:* This is perhaps the most powerful form of nuclear fuel. When you release free reports based on comprehensive research, you can achieve amazing benefits. By surveying people in your industry and presenting the results in an easy-to-read report, you can become a thought leader very

FIGURE 1.4 Nuclear fuel quickly moves your business toward its destinations.

quickly. SocialMediaExaminer.com releases a free annual *Social Media Marketing Industry Report* that is typically read by 40,000 people in a matter of days.

◆ *Top 10 contests:* Remember, people crave recognition. Top 10 contests typically seek nominations and ask people to vote for their favorite company, blog, book, or any other category. Conducting a well-executed top 10 contest can attract power players to your company and lead to remarkable exposure. Back when I started SocialMediaExaminer.com, we conducted a Top 10 Social Media Blogs contest that helped get our name on the map in a major way.

◆ *White papers:* These are educational documents designed to help persuade people about a concept, product, or service. They tend to average 6 to 10 pages in length and address trends, problems, and solutions. Unique from other forms of nuclear fuel, white papers can have a very long propulsion period. For example, a white paper I wrote in 2006 has brought in more than 85,000 leads and is still delivering 30 each day.

◆ *Micro events:* Webinars, teleclasses, social media events, and live video broadcasts are examples of micro events. These free events typically are one hour in duration and bring an expert of some kind live to your audience. They are more powerful than expert interviews because they are live, rotate around a space and time, and attract many people. They also provide excellent exposure to the expert. A great example is Sam Rosen's "The Influencer Project." He invited 60 thought leaders to deliver 60-second messages over one hour; 5,500 people attended the live event.

Generating nuclear fuel does, however, require a major effort. But using only a few nuclear bursts will help differentiate your company from the competition in a dramatic way.

■ ■ ■

Using primary and nuclear fuel—the great content that will propel your business—is absolutely essential to helping your rocket gain forward momentum. In later chapters in this book, I will reveal precisely how to create these types of content, and what to avoid, ensuring your business ongoing success.

OTHER PEOPLE

Fuel gets your rocket ship moving, but people determine where it goes.

A key distinction of the elevation principle involves doing great things for people *outside of your business*, many of whom will likely never become customers. Simply said, give to others—constantly—and your business will quickly grow.

This idea may seem counterintuitive. Perhaps you're thinking, "Why should I waste energy on people who have no interest in my success?" Or maybe you're wondering, "Why should I help someone who's never done anything for me?" These are good questions to ask, questions I've also chewed on.

Over the years I've realized that *most people couldn't care less about my business*. They don't walk around all day wondering how they can help me. In fact, they're so caught up in their daily activities that I'm not even on their radar.

I learned this the hard way. At first I figured people would be willing to do things just because I asked. I also thought they'd buy my products just because I crafted a good sales page.

My first paid job was delivering a weekly newspaper as a young kid in Wisconsin. Each month my boss asked me to go door-to-door and sell people a small yellow card with two coupons on it. Yes, he asked me to sell coupons!

So I went knocking. Occasionally I'd get the "Oh, you're such a nice young boy—here's a few dollars for your coupons." But most people slammed the door in my face. I knew they couldn't care less about the cheesy coupons.

Frankly, that job didn't last very long. But I learned an important lesson: that *asking people for money often results in repeated rejection.*

Many, many years later, the revelation came. Long after I had cut my teeth in sales and marketing, I discovered a better way to sell. I realized that *if I simply did great things for other people, I didn't really need to ask for their help.* If I did for others precisely what I wanted them to do for me, perhaps something might change.

I discovered that *most people find great value when others help them solve their problems* and when they achieve recognition for their accomplishments.

My thinking was all backward: *Rather than looking for people who would bend to my will, I needed to bend my will to people.* Instead of asking, "What have you done for me lately?," I needed to ask myself, "What have I done for you lately?"

This marked a paradigm shift in my thinking.

People love receiving genuine gifts. They love it when others recognize their hard work, help promote their content, or reach out to help without asking for anything in return. So I shifted my mind-set to: "Who can I help?" Then things took off.

Here are the different types of people who can play into your business growth:

- ◆ *Your base:* Your objective should be to build a base of people on which you can build your business. These are readers of your blog, subscribers to your content, fans of your social media sites, and so on. Your gift to these people is the continuous delivery of great content that helps them solve their problems, with no strings attached. You can also give gifts by promptly answering their many questions and recognizing those individuals who exhibit exemplary participation with others in your base.

◆ *Outside experts:* Seek out people that your base would be interested in and shine the spotlight on them. This could include book authors, successful peers, or known industry experts. Activities you could perform for experts might include an interview, a case study of their businesses, or a review of their books, products, or services. Your gift to the experts is exposure to your base. Your gift to your base is sharing tips from the experts and showing them what success can look like.

◆ *Fire starters:* These are superexperts who have raving fan bases. Often their actions can ignite a domino effect that can take your business to new heights. Just being associated with these people can have a positive impact on your brand.

So how does helping others propel your business?

◆ It *eliminates the perception of the pitch*. People have very advanced sales-pitch detectors. When you provide value to other people, they'll see your business in a different light.

◆ When you're close with people, *you'll see trends*. Helping people with their problems provides valuable market research, enables you to anticipate trends, and helps you manage change.

◆ Providing genuine gifts to others also *expands your base*. People love sharing great content and love propping up businesses that they find truly helpful.

◆ Carefully targeting experts also *leads to strategic partnerships*. If you target the right people with access to a much larger base than your own, you could find yourself partnering in a way that benefits both of your businesses.

◆ Helping others *greatly reduces rejection*. Oftentimes, people I've helped have turned the tables on me and asked me how they could help me—unsolicited. And when the time came when I needed help, they nearly always were willing to assist.

◆ Helping people *ensures your business will stand out from the competition.* While the rest of your industry is focused on taking money from people, you'll be focused on enriching people who can become evangelists for your business, and many will gladly give you their money down the road.

The American Express OPEN Forum provides a platform for small business owners. Many high-profile experts pen original content on the OpenForum.com site. By combining great content and other people, American Express is able to attract many people to its site with the hope that some will decide to sign up for an American Express card.

To build a base and engage other experts, you'll need a strategy to ensure your content is getting in front of the right people, that you're retaining and growing your base, and that you know how to build relationships that lead to strong partnerships. In later chapters of this book, I will show you precisely how to do this.

Once you have fuel and a base of people, the next step is to tone down your sales and marketing efforts.

No Obvious Marketing Messages—At First

I was at a large trade show in Las Vegas. I had just wrapped up an on-camera interview with a rather well-known marketing executive. After thanking me for the interview, he asked, "How can I help you?"

I thought to myself, "Wow, this guy gets it. What a brilliant first question to ask me." After I replied, "I can't think of anything off the top of my head, but thank you," he said something else—which, unfortunately fully erased the goodwill of his previous gesture.

He proceeded to spout a litany of things he wanted from me, including a book review, promotional activities, and so on. I politely smiled and said to myself, "No way."

His tactical error was revealing his cards too early. He chose the road of efficiency and—unknown to him—he hit a dead end. I had just given him a gift (the interview) and he asked for much more—almost immediately.

Now, in his defense, I admit I've done the same thing before. I just didn't know any better back then. Perhaps you've done this as well?

This story demonstrates how many businesses get marketing wrong. To use a hunter analogy, *businesses are going for the quick kill because the target is in sight.* But if the hunter owns the land where the deer live, there'll be another day to bag the prey. Simply said, they'll be back and they'll be bigger. Marketers need to stop hunting and start focusing on building places customers want to frequent.

The final component in the elevation principle is to *eliminate your marketing messages*—or at least the perception of them.

Your goal should be to grow your base and your relationships with experts *before* you worry about cranking up the sales and marketing engines.

Think of marketing like friction: The more you use it, the slower your rocket ship will move. If you overdo it, you'll experience no forward momentum—and that can be disastrous (see Figure 1.5).

Less marketing makes your rocket ship much larger by growing your base.

FIGURE 1.5 Businesses that overemphasize marketing messages rarely leave the atmosphere. Those that focus on great content and other people travel at warp speed.

In the context of great content, *blatant or frequent marketing messages simply say to people you're all about the sale.* It changes their opinion. It engages their distrust engines. And when those engines rev up, your future customers are gone.

Too much marketing is like endless flashing neon lights that shout "Buy Now." People see those signs and ignore them. They also distrust businesses that overload them with marketing messages. In contrast, *when you remove most or all marketing messages, you can come across as a very valuable resource and begin forward momentum.*

Let me illustrate this from my own experience. When I launched SocialMediaExaminer.com I made the decision not to advertise or sell any products or services until we had at least 10,000 e-mail subscribers. Some might argue this was a costly and shortsighted decision. "You're leaving money on the table," others have said. But I knew it was the right thing to do.

My goal was to recruit valuable experts to contribute original content to the site. I knew that if it *appeared I was financially profiting from other people's content, it could deter their commitment.*

I also knew that when new people came to our site, and saw the great content authored by knowledgeable experts, they'd be more impressed if there was absolutely nothing for sale.

So I made the strategic decision to make SocialMediaExaminer .com a *movement,* something people wanted to be part of. I greatly deemphasized my role. Instead, I gave a commercial-free stage to other experts. And people rushed in by the tens of thousands.

After only a few weeks, Technorati ranked us as one of the world's top 5 small business blogs. Six months into the launch, we had more than 100,000 people visiting the site monthly and 20,000 e-mail subscribers.

When we finally turned on the marketing engines, we had a blockbuster experience, generating nearly a million dollars from a single event.

By eliminating all perceptions of marketing, our rocket ship— propelled by tons of people—shot into outer space. We did slow down the growth of our base to do some marketing when the time was right—and that was always the plan. Had we been marketing from the beginning, we would have been much smaller and much less successful.

There's always a place for some marketing. It's just not so obvious. You should be constantly employing what I call *"under-the-radar" forms of marketing.* These techniques involve ensuring your great content shows up in front of the right people, capturing the names and e-mails of people, and growing your following, while leaving selling for some time in the future.

There's also a time and place for traditional marketing. Your business needs to sell to survive, so don't forgo marketing forever. When intense marketing is employed, you'll experience a stall in the growth of your base, and typically your content production (your fuel) will be hindered. The keys to success involve knowing *when to flip the marketing levers fully on* and *when to shut them off.* Later in the book I will explore these concepts in detail.

When the right content is supported by the right people, and the marketing engines are off (eliminating drag), the elevation principle can propel your business to new heights.

Why the Formula Works

Why does great content matter? Do you really need great people? And can you get by with the marketing engines always on? Why must these three ideas work together?

Let me use the movie industry as an example. An incredible movie with a really stellar storyline may never make it to your town because it lacks the name recognition of a known actor and support of a major studio. It might be seen in a few random places, but will likely never become the blockbuster it could have been.

Similarly, you might be able to produce outstanding content. But if the right people do not see that content, what impact is it having on your business?

Back in 2006, I was a new blogger focused on empowering other writers by sharing tips on how to craft content and market it. I had a rather small following. The biggest blog in my world was Copyblogger .com, run by Brian Clark. I reached out to Brian and asked if he'd be willing to let me write an article for his site. He said sure.

I put together a nice post and it went live on Copyblogger.com. The response from Brian's audience was off the charts. It led to me landing a nice gig from one of his readers, and it opened my eyes.

I learned that *good content really does matter*. But *where the content resides* is just as important. Because Copyblogger had a huge base of people who matched my ideal readers, writing for Brian's site was a wise move for my business. I gained the exposure and the support of a power player. Thus, great content in front of the right people is essential.

Why? Because *good content is often shared*, giving you further exposure. It is e-mailed, printed, bookmarked, tweeted, and shared on Facebook. If you can *expand the size of your reachable audience, you can increase the share factor.* More of the right people reading your content and sharing it will help you achieve great success.

In a perfect world, you own the platform where your content resides, but that's not necessary, as the Copyblogger.com example illustrates.

The power of great people goes much further. In the case of Copyblogger.com, I continued to write for Brian's site. I gave him a gift in the process, as well. My writing was popular and helped attract more people to the site.

Eventually, I asked Brian if he'd be willing to participate in an event I was organizing. He said yes without hesitation. Having his big name associated with my event brought in a lot more sales. It led to a good relationship that has been very profitable for both of our businesses.

Great content in front of a great audience and with the support of experts can really go places, opening many opportunities for your business. But do you really need to tone down the marketing messages?

To address this, I'm going to take a page from my white paper playbook. I've written for many of the world's largest companies. I faced strenuous objections when crafting persuasive white papers. My clients often asked why I was so insistent on not mentioning the name of the company until the last page. I often heard objections like, "We need this piece to produce sales," or "That's not how we've always done it."

Here's what I told businesses the likes of FedEx, Dow Jones, and Microsoft. *The moment you stop mentioning your products and services by name is the moment you shift from being a salesperson to being an advocate.*

Remember, everyone wants access to great insight and great people, *before* they want great products and services.

By simply abstracting out the brand, a business can move the mental bar in people's brains from "I'm being sold," to "I'm being educated."

In the same way, when businesses can move the marketing messages to the background, they can help ensure their content is *fully received and valued by people.*

When outstanding content is coupled with great people, and decoupled from marketing messages, your business can quickly attract a larger base, more partnership opportunities, and significantly more sales.

■　■　■

Now that you understand the core underpinnings of the elevation principle and how it can be used, it's important to spend some time examining how to get your business flying. You have a lot of competition. To ensure your rocket ship is headed in the right direction, you need a mission plan. The next chapter reveals precisely how to map out your flight plan.

Starting Your Mission Plan

But why, some say, the moon? Why choose this as our goal? And they may as well ask why climb the highest mountain?
—John F. Kennedy, May 1961

D o you know where you want to go? In the summer of 1969, more than eight years after President Kennedy declared the United States would land a man on the moon, Apollo 11 took flight in a historic event. Yes, at least eight years of planning went into this mission.

Prior to this accomplishment, the United States had launched men into space four other times in preparation for the big event. Through systematic tests and modifications, the National Aeronautics and Space Administration (NASA) was able to accomplish what seemed impossible only a few years earlier.

NASA didn't expect to land on the moon in their earlier missions. In fact, that was never the goal. Instead, they were constantly improving, in preparation for their ultimate mission.

What can space travel teach you about marketing and business growth? A lot. Similar to the concepts in the elevation principle, there's a time and a place for everything. And the chances of launching your business into outer space without planning are about zero.

In this chapter, I'll help you create a mission plan using the elements of the elevation principle discussed in Chapter 1. We'll examine concepts like determining your vision, creating content goals, and setting a trajectory.

Establishing Your Clear Vision

"We choose to go to the moon in this decade and do the other things, not because they are easy, but because they are hard, because that goal will serve to organize and measure the best of our energies and skills, because that challenge is one that we are willing to accept, one we are unwilling to postpone, and one which we intend to win," said John F. Kennedy.[1]

If the United States didn't have the vision of reaching the moon, it wouldn't have been able to set a course that ultimately led it there.

What's your vision? This may seem like a no-brainer concept, but it's very easy to lose focus and drift off into space without a clear vision.

You wouldn't pack your suitcase for a trip without first knowing where you're headed, would you? Then why do so many of us (including myself) forget where we're headed while operating our businesses? We forget to pack a change of winter clothes and find our businesses unprepared for the likely blizzards ahead.

Early in my career I was a freelance copywriter who helped businesses craft marketing messages. I was pretty clueless about vision. All I knew was that I had a service other people were willing to pay for.

Over time I found myself expanding to include design services like Web site creation and animation. I didn't really care what I was doing as long as the demand for my services was there.

Eventually, I found my business in an unfamiliar place. My focus was far from writing and more reliant on expensive and complicated design projects. My rocket ship had drifted off its original course.

Then one day, the economy shifted and many of my large clients stopped purchasing my services. Demand died. I found my rocket ship stalled in the middle of a major storm.

I had no vision and no trajectory. I had let the cosmic jet streams of demand push my business in unfamiliar directions—and I was stuck. Have you had a similar experience?

Had I been like NASA and had a clear idea of where I was headed, things might have been different.

Here's how to establish your vision.

---

[1] Speech given at Rice University, Houston, Texas, September 12, 1962.

WHAT'S YOUR VISION?

Where do you want to go? *A vision statement is a simple sentence or two that helps keep you focused during moments of uncertainty.* It's a clear picture you can see in your head, one that guides your every decision.

Establishing a vision is important because it helps ensure you keep your business headed in the right direction.

Vision has played an important role in the success of businesses and individuals for decades.

"Gaining a clear and precise vision was what catapulted John D. Rockefeller from a ten-cents-an-hour bookkeeper to the richest man in the world. It transformed Helen Keller from a bitter young girl into one of the most inspirational speakers and writers of all time. It became the driving force that empowered Ray Kroc to look at a single tiny restaurant in San Bernardino, California, and transform it into the 25,000-franchise restaurant system of today's McDonald's," explained Steven K. Scott.[2]

A clear vision paints a desirable future. It should be big enough that it guides every decision your business makes.

You can start your vision statement simply by asking this question: "Where do I ultimately want my business to be?"

Here are two examples of vision statements from large brands:

Southwest Airlines:

Our vision is to expand our locations both domestic and overseas by being the largest and most profitable airline company, to achieve both short- and long-haul carriers efficiently and with low cost. Also to be an airline carrier that has the most productive workforce, to guarantee the best flight possible for each and every passenger.[3]

Nike:

To bring inspiration and innovation to every athlete in the world.*

* If you have a body, you are an athlete.[4]

---

[2] Scott, K.S. *The Richest Man Who Ever Lived: King Solomon's Secrets to Success, Wealth, and Happiness* (New York: Crown Business, 2006).

[3] Dow, M., Belanger, K., and Bourgoin, A. Southwest Airlines Co. Presentation, 2004. www.scribd.com/doc/35159128/Southwest-Airlines-1.

[4] Nikebiz.com. Company overview, 2010.

In the case of Southwest Airlines, its vision would clearly help the company expand outside the United States, strive to lower expenses, and invest in programs that ensured the best possible customer service.

The Nike vision would justify the company attempting to sponsor every athlete possible, in some way. It would also guide decisions to invest in athletic programs in developing nations.

In the case of NASA, the vision of landing on the moon justified the development of technology needed to accomplish their mission. The results of their innovation we take for granted today, including cordless power tools, shoe insoles, long-distance wireless communications, freeze-dried food, water purification, CAT scanning, and much more.

Clear vision statements also help businesses say no to projects that are off-mission. For example, had NASA been faced with limited resources and a choice between studying the rings of Saturn versus the atmosphere of the moon, the decision would have been very easy.

Had my copywriting business had a vision of creating written content, I might not have been pulled into complicated design projects that nearly led to the demise of my business.

The two vision statement examples also show how a simple sentence or two can guide future business decisions. Here are some other examples I made up:

- My vision is to become the world's most recognized musical talent agent, seeking to discover emerging talent and transform them into superstars.
- We want to be the nation's largest provider of nutritional supplements while offering the highest levels of customer satisfaction.
- Our park seeks to become the state's most popular destination and inspire tourists to make lasting memories from their experiences here.

Now that you've been exposed to some vision examples, it's time to craft your own business vision.

How to Create Your Vision

Get yourself in a quiet place where you can think. Your future is important, so make the time to clear your head.

When I need to think, I like to get in my car and head out to the edge of town where there are no distractions. Bring a clipboard and a pen. Turn off all distractions. Now turn on your mind.

Promise yourself you'll commit at least 60 minutes of quality time to working on your vision. In reality, that hour will just get you started. You'll likely need to carve out some more time for a few days until you come up with a clear vision.

When crafting your vision, ask yourself the following questions:

◆ What do I want to achieve?
◆ Where do I want to go?
◆ Why do I want it? What are my underlying motivations?
◆ Can others rally around my vision?
◆ What perceived problems am I addressing?

Write down the answers to these questions.

Spend some time thinking about your vision. What does it look like once you've accomplished it? What kind of opportunities will exist? What kind of influence will your business have?

Now step back into the present and focus on these two questions:

◆ What am I lacking today?
◆ What can keep me from accomplishing my vision?

The last two questions shouldn't stop you from coming up with your vision. Instead, they should clarify your vision by identifying areas of weakness you'll need to plan for. For example, are you lacking knowledge, finances, or access to influential people?

Spend time working on your vision. Jot down your ideas. Try to develop your vision into a single sentence or two. Keep refining it. The most compelling vision statements are often a simple phrase.

Is your vision something you can see? Can you actually visualize your business achieving the vision down the road?

Once you feel you have a strong vision, test it with your peers. Make further refinements as needed. Then finalize the vision. Print it out. Paste it on your wall. Look at it daily.

If you want to discover more about how to create a strong vision, check out the vision mapping concepts discussed in Steven K. Scott's book, *The Richest Man Who Ever Lived.*

Once you have established a clear vision for your business, determine the steps needed to reach it. I like to call those steps your shorter-term goals.

Crafting Measurable Goals

Goals are those milestones you reach on your journey toward your vision. They help you know you're making progress and enable you to course-correct if things aren't turning out as you planned.

NASA knew how many miles it was to the moon and how fast the Apollo spacecraft could reasonably travel. Similarly, you should identify a goal and how long it should take your business to achieve it.

Unique from a longer-term vision, goals should be focused on shorter-term outcomes that you can easily quantify. *Tie content and other people, two core elements of the elevation principle, into your goals.*

Your goals should be:

Specific: Be as precise as you can with your goals. Rather than saying, "We want more customers," document what kind of customers you are seeking. Try to address the who, what, where, and when questions with your goals. For example: "Before the end of the year, we want to build strategic relationships with at least two experts who have written *New York Times* bestselling books."

Measurable: If you can't measure your goals, you'll never know if you've reached them. Numbers and dates are the keys to measurement. Make sure your goals have one (or both) of these to be measurable. For example: "In the next 12 months, our business will publish six pieces of original content in third-party publications with at least 15,000 subscribers." With this goal you can easily measure progress.

Attainable: While you should push your business further with your goals, they must be attainable. Unrealistic goals will only discourage you. Know the limits of your company and your time, then select goals that are fully attainable. For example, if part of your marketing strategy is to produce white papers, make sure you understand the time that it takes to produce each one. It would be very unrealistic to release a white paper every month without the proper resources. However, once a quarter might be an attainable goal for your business.

Relevant: Ask yourself, "Are our goals pushing us closer to our vision?" If they're not, they might not be worth pursuit. Learning to say no is just as important as planning attainable goals. When large projects are about to be tackled by your organization, always go back to your vision statement. Irrelevant goals are perhaps one of the biggest reasons businesses find themselves off course.

Time-bound: It's important to work toward deadlines. Set your business goals down on the calendar. Many businesses use major trade shows to spur the execution of ideas. The more specific you can be with dates, the easier it will be to stop putting off what needs to be done. Mark Twain was known for saying, "Never put off until tomorrow what you can do the day after tomorrow." When you force a deadline on a goal, you'll be able to overcome the innate desire to procrastinate that Twain alluded to.

The management-consulting world calls these attributes SMART goal setting. These types of goals are smart for your business because they become understandable and actionable.

Said another way, smart goals must address the following questions:

◆ Are they really specific?
◆ Can I measure them?
◆ How do I know I'm actually achieving my goals?
◆ Are they not so pie-in-the-sky that I can actually attain them?
◆ Are my goals relevant to my vision?
◆ Are they on a schedule? Do I have them on my calendar?

EXAMPLES OF SMART GOALS

When I was planning for the launch of SocialMediaExaminer.com I had a few specific goals I wanted to achieve. Here are two of them:

◆ *Forty thousand e-mail subscribers within 12 months:* This was a very aggressive goal, but I knew it was achievable, based on the hot topic of social media and experience with my prior businesses. I made sure to carefully track the monthly growth rate of subscribers. On our first birthday we achieved our goal. Because the goal was crystal clear, there were times I needed to implement special promotional campaigns to ensure we reached that number.

◆ *Become the number-two social media blog within a year:* I knew this was also a very aggressive goal, considering how many bloggers focus on social media. Mashable.com is one of the world's top three blogs and I knew it was fully unrealistic to expect to beat them. So I recruited bright up-and-coming bloggers, like Jay Baer of ConvinceAndConvert.com, to author monthly columns, and brought unique original content to the world of social media. I also focused on longer-form magazine-style content, unique from Mashable's news-focused shorter content. Within months of our launch, our name was used along with Mashable as the top two destinations for social media content.

These two examples demonstrate how SMART goals can really drive your business toward success.

WHEN TO CREATE YOUR GOALS

In the context of other people and content, you may find it difficult to determine specific goals without first reading additional chapters of this book. In later chapters I will address how to find other people and how to craft content. I suggest you come back to this chapter after you've determined the mix of content you'd like to pursue.

Once you set achievable goals that are easily measurable, and align with your vision, it will be much easier to set your trajectory.

Setting Your Course Trajectory

Think of your vision as your future destination and your goals as what keeps you motivated to move forward toward the vision. If you were to lay out everything on paper (which I suggest you do), you should be able to set a course to success.

Your trajectory is a clear path your business can follow to reach the vision. It's like a connect-the-dots puzzle that takes you right to your destination. Content and other people fuel your movement toward goals.

Similar to space travel, *objects are constantly in motion in the business world.* If you were to hop into a hypothetical spacecraft and head straight to the moon, it would be gone by the time you arrived. Had you taken into account that the moon orbits around the earth every 27 days or so, you would have been able to set a course ahead of the moon. Thus, you would have arrived right as the moon spun into your orbit.

In the context of business, you need to *look forward and predict how your goals might be shifting based on market factors.* For example, if you're targeting an up-and-coming industry expert for a longer-term strategic relationship, you'll need to calculate how long it will take that relationship to form and where that person might be on his or her own growth path. The hope is that you'll come along at the right moment and be able to help that person in a way that benefits him or her.

Earlier in this chapter I mentioned that I recruited Jay Baer to write a monthly column for SocialMediaExaminer.com. I saw that he was very talented and articulate. I met him at a conference, and he impressed me. I looked at his blog and was blown away by his writing.

I knew he was in the beginning stages of his growth, based on the size of his audience. So I offered him a monthly column on our site. It turned out to be a good choice. Jay went on to develop a speaking platform, and co-authored a popular book called *The Now Revolution: 7 Shifts to Make Your Business Faster, Smarter, and More Social* (Wiley, 2011).

In the case of SocialMediaExaminer.com, part of our trajectory involved finding the next Jay Baers of the world and connecting with them before they exploded in popularity.

Let's take a deeper look at what's involved with a trajectory.

THE COMPONENTS OF TRAJECTORY

Setting a trajectory for your business involves markers, speed, and motion. Let me explain each of these concepts:

Markers: The equivalent of space buoys, markers are key accomplishments that lead your business to its goals. Markers are the dots on the space map you'll be following. They'll help you stay on course. They are your daily and weekly to-do tasks.

Speed: Your business naturally operates at different speeds. As you approach key goals, you'll likely speed up to accomplish them on schedule. After you've achieved your goals, the business will naturally slow down for a period. Tracking the changing speed at which you must move to accomplish your shorter-term missions is important to ensuring you stay on track. Other people help determine the speed of your business progress.

Motion: Also known as *forward thrust*, your business must be constantly moving to ensure it remains in flight. Achieving motion requires burning your content fuel and performing activities. This means creating the right content and performing the tasks needed to reach your markers.

Here's how to visualize these three concepts together:

1. Imagine a sheet of paper with three large dots drawn on it, from bottom to top. Each of those dots represents markers.
2. Now draw a line from each marker to the next. That line represents speed, or the time it takes you to get from marker to marker.
3. Finally, grab a coin, place it on the bottom marker and start moving it up the line. The work you're doing to push that coin up the line is motion. Motion is fueled by great content and the speed at which you move is controlled by other people. The coin represents your business, and the effort of your finger represents the tasks and content you've employed.

Let's put this into practice.

Recall that a key goal of SocialMediaExaminer.com was growing to 40,000 e-mail subscribers in 12 months.

We set a series of markers in place to help ensure we arrived at that goal. One of our first steps was to move from three articles per week to five. Outstanding content was critical to our growth. We knew the more we published, the faster we'd grow.

We needed 20 writers to achieve our publishing goals. We established an active recruitment process seeking new content contributors.

This involved me reaching out to key people I knew and inviting them to participate. The pitch was simple: You write one original article a month for us and gain amazing exposure from our rapidly growing base. They had witnessed the early success and knew my track record.

Goals sometimes shift due to market factors. After a month or so, we realized that managing 20 different writers had become difficult. Some weren't able to meet the schedule. Others weren't living up to our editorial standards. We decided to put a general call out to our readers, seeking quality writers. We quickly expanded to more than 50 regular content contributors.

Retaining a large base of ongoing writers was just one of our markers, which mapped into our bigger goal of 40,000 subscribers. Another one involved developing techniques that encouraged new visitors to subscribe to our daily e-mail newsletters. Yet another involved making it easy for existing subscribers to encourage their friends to sign up for our e-mails.

And as you can see, a series of markers was put in place to help us reach our goal of 40,000 subscribers. Because our goal was set to a date, we knew we could easily look at our monthly subscriber growth to determine if we needed to increase our speed.

Thus, some of our markers to grow to 40,000 subscribers included recruiting 20 new writers, then recruiting 30 more, publishing 5 days a week, developing e-mail capture methods, and implementing a "suggest to a friend" system. When these markers were documented, our trajectory was easy to follow.

Having a vision and goals is only half the battle. Many businesses drop the proverbial ball by not coming up with the actual action plan needed to achieve their goals. This is where laying down markers, calculating the speed at which your business can move, and deter-mining what motions (or actions) are needed to move the business forward come into play.

Here are two more concepts worth exploration.

Gravity drag: Depending where you are along your trajectory, you may experience gravity drag. These are forces that work against your forward movement. They may include unforeseen events, strong competitive threats, fear, poor planning, or general uncertainty about your mission plan. Often, gravity drag occurs at the beginning of a launch.

Escape velocity: To overcome gravity drag, your business must understand *escape velocity*. This occurs when your business speeds up fast enough to enter into outer space, where there is no gravity. The key to achieving escape velocity is gaining the assistance of other people who can help quickly propel your business.

Gravity drag and escape velocity are at play against each other. Gravity wants to hold you down. You escape its grip once you achieve great momentum.

Here are examples of how each has played into my business ventures.

A few years back I spend $2,000 on an Internet marketing guru's online course. I wanted to learn how to gain control of people so they'd simply purchase my products like crazy.

This marketer made it all sound so easy, and the outcome so certain. Using this system, I spent serious hours putting together a program that I'd later release to the world. I even called my credit card merchant and asked that my account be upgraded by a million dollars—I was that certain of the results.

I followed this guy's model to the letter. I created a great series of content that I would be selling. I also crafted all the marketing content designed to lure in the masses.

After spending a hundred-plus hours in preparation, I launched my program. I was certain the dollars would be flowing in like a river.

Actually, only a light drizzle was the result. I made only 40 sales, about 960 shy of my goal. And to make matters worse, nearly half asked for a refund. It was a horrendous experience.

All along, I was really uncomfortable with the methods I was using. I was following the leadership of a guru (I thought), so I moved forward despite my reluctance. I let the thrill of a quick buck get in the way of my normal way of doing business.

In this case, my gravity drag was caused by a lack of checking the methods against my audience's expectations and my own comfort level. The whole experience really brought my business down in a crippling way. This is the negative power of gravity drag.

Here's the positive power of escape velocity:

After the dust settled in this situation, I took a hard look at what went wrong. I had learned a lot of lessons and had created some really outstanding content. So I pondered, "What if I could take what I learned and put a new spin on it?"

I took the idea of delivering great content and decided to take it live. Instead of just me teaching it, I reached out to my peers. I decided to launch an online event called the Copywriting Success Summit. I recruited folks like Bob Bly (author, *The Copywriter's Handbook: A Step-by-Step Guide to Writing Copy That Sells*; Holt Paperbacks, 1990), Peter Bowerman (author, *The Well-Fed Writer: Financial Self-Sufficiency as a Commercial Freelancer in Six Months or Less*; Fanove Publishing, 2nd ed., 2009), Steve Slaunwhite (author, *Start & Run a Copywriting Business*; Self-Counsel Press; 2nd ed., 2005), and Brian Clark (founder of Copyblogger.com) to participate.

There was no less work involved this time. However, the team of power players made this a different experience.

The launch went off well. We ended up selling 364 tickets. More important, 99 percent of attendees said they'd recommend the event to a friend. The response from attendees was off the charts.

In a postevent debrief, Steve Slaunwhite suggested I do more of these kinds of events, and that I'd found my sweet spot. I took his advice.

My business went on to offer more Success Summits related to copywriting, white papers, social media, Facebook marketing, and blogging. Now each event sells thousands of tickets—and the sky's the limit. These events became the largest online conferences in their respective industries.

In this case, I was able to achieve escape velocity, with the assistance of powerful industry peers and while working within my comfort zone.

This example demonstrates the power of escape velocity. Once your business overcomes the forces of gravity drag, you enter into outer space—a place rarely seen by your competitors.

Combining the right markers at the right speed with forward motion, while avoiding gravity drag, is essential to moving your business toward its vision.

CONNECTING THE DOTS

Your ultimate goal is to write down all the goals you need to achieve to get your business to its vision, and then lay down detailed markers, paving a path along which you can move your business.

I learned the following technique while in college: *Start with the end in mind and work backward.* Imagine you have already arrived. Then ask yourself, how did I get here?

Begin by going back one single step from having achieved your vision, and ask yourself, "Which action step got my business here?" Keep asking, "What did I do just before that?" Continue working your way backward, all the way to the present.

Tell yourself you've already accomplished your vision. Now document how it happened, working in reverse.

In the case of NASA, landing a man on the moon might have involved the following goals (listed in reverse order):

    4. Have a man walk on the moon.
    3. Navigate successful landing and takeoff from the moon.
    2. Orbit the moon.
    1. Leave and reenter earth's atmosphere.

Each of these goals might have been a planned mission. If each mission were accomplished, NASA would be one step closer to its true vision of landing a man on the moon.

In between each of these goals was a series of markers that led to the next goal. For example, to go from landing a spacecraft on the moon to allowing a man to step out on the moon likely took a series of technological developments. Some might have included testing the surface of the moon to ensure it could support a man, designing moon shoes, creating a protective suit, and so on.

Here's another example: Assume you've accomplished your vision of becoming the world's leading white-paper authority. These might have been the key goals that got you to your vision, again, organized backward:

    10. Be declared world's leading expert by many peers.
    9. Teach courses at major corporations.
    8. Train fellow writers how to craft white papers at my own events.

7. Speak annually at large national trade shows in the fields of marketing and writing.
6. Write a bestselling book.
5. Craft 100 white papers for world's biggest brands.
4. Launch a popular blog.
3. Build a leading Web portal for writers and marketers of white papers.
2. Publish a monthly newsletter to 10,000 subscribers.
1. Create a free how-to white paper that helps build a base.

The beauty of this backward goal-setting method is that it lays out a step-by-step trajectory your business can follow. Simply by asking a question such as, "How did I get to teaching courses at major corporations?" you can lay out an entire action plan with critical markers.

The preceding example is real. It was the game plan I came up with after my copywriting business failed. I decided to focus on white papers, and followed the plan just itemized. I was determined not to repeat my bad habits.

In your case, *the more details you can add to your trajectory, the better.*

Underneath each of your accomplishments on your own action plan, you should document detailed markers. For example, using item number 1 in my list—creating a how-to white paper—you could come up with the following actions:

1. Determine topic.
2. Identify ideal reader and objective of paper.
3. Draft outline.
4. Write paper.
5. Determine marketing strategy.
6. Create landing page.

Use this technique to write out the precise trajectory for your business. Tack it up on your wall. Look at it regularly. Be sure to course-correct if your business is going in the wrong direction. And watch out for gravity drag.

■ ■ ■

This chapter examined the importance of establishing a detailed vision and clear goals. It also examined how to develop markers and place them on a trajectory, while avoiding gravity drag. Once your vision, goals, and trajectory are clear, it's helpful to identify role models that can spur inspiration and seek out great content and people. These topics will be addressed in the next chapter.

Finding Inspiration by Looking Outward

People never improve unless they look to some standard or example higher and better than themselves.

—Tryon Edwards

What are your sources of inspiration? It was the Soviet Union's 1957 launch of the unmanned satellite Sputnik that motivated the U.S. space program to successfully launch Explorer 1 the following year. A space race was under way.

Years later, NASA head Michael Griffin explained the U.S. reaction to Sputnik: "We felt that we were falling behind in our much-vaunted technical know-how and industrial capability. The small metal orb beeping overhead, visible in the clear fall sky to anyone who looked—and nearly everyone did—reminded us of this."[1]

Had the United States not been watching, it wouldn't have been spurred to create plans to land the first man on the moon.

What are you watching?

---

[1] Lemos, R. "Sputnik Stunned the World, and Its Rocket Scared the Pentagon," *Wired*, October 3, 2007. www.wired.com/science/space/news/2007/10/sputnik_anniversary.

An outward-focused mind-set provides an important source of inspiration for businesses. When you look for inspiration outside the walls of your business, you'll find endless ideas.

This outward focus can serve as a powerful catalyst that unites your company to strive toward its vision and goals. Even more importantly, *looking outward will inspire the content creation process and help identify other people who may be instrumental to your business growth*.

Content is fuel for your business, and other people control the speed of your progress. Without the proper systems in place, your rocket ship will need to constantly stop for fuel, slowing your forward progress. However, by following the procedures outlined in this chapter, you'll have ongoing access to fuel and people, ensuring your ship doesn't stall.

Is your business looking outside its rocket ship windows? What (and who) are you watching?

You'll find amazing inspiration when you look to other people, businesses, and written works. But you must look.

Seek out new ideas. Watch for them. When you look carefully at the success of others, you'll find new ways to grow your business.

This chapter will help you add key processes to your mission plan that will speed you toward your vision. You'll discover how to identify role models, find inspirational content, build an idea vault, and establish a content and people discovery system.

Identifying Role Models

I've found it exceptionally helpful to watch creativity at work in other people—especially those outside my own industry. Role models are those people you look at and say, "That person is really doing it right."

If you can find a good business leader, and model some of your business activities after that person's methods, you'll be less likely to fail. You'll gain a significant jump start if you find the right role models.

For example, when I decided to focus on writing white papers as a new business, I happened across the work of Andrew Goodman. He had crafted an exceptional ebook on Google advertising (back when Google AdWords were just becoming popular) called, *21 Ways to Maximize ROI on Google AdWords Select*. I loved his informative ebook.

I was also intrigued by the way he used content. I carefully watched everything he did. I noticed he had a blog. He also published rich e-mail newsletters exclusively for the folks who purchased his products.

I started asking myself, "If I can find such value in what Andrew is doing, how can I provide similar value to my base?" I attribute a lot of my early ideas to watching and modeling Andrew.

Who are your role models?

FINDING ROLE MODELS

You might be thinking, "I don't know anyone or any business that I'd consider a role model." The good news is there are plenty of role models available to you.

Watch for those people that others can't stop talking about. When many people are singing the praises of someone (or some company), that person (or company) might have the makings of a role model.

I'd suggest you *start by looking outside your industry*. Your role models could be from any professional arena. This means you'll likely need to think a little outside the box.

If you're used to reading magazines and blogs that cover only your marketplace, try looking in a totally different space. For example, if you're a management consultant, try seeking out self-improvement gurus for inspiration. Alternatively, if you sell industrial chemicals to businesses, maybe you should be watching consumer brands like Clorox for ideas.

Role models can be individual people or brands. And you might find inspiration in unexpected locations and situations. I found Andrew Goodman only because I needed to understand Google advertising. Little did I expect him to become a role model.

Try to find a person, or a couple of people, you can track. Then carefully watch what they do. Read their blogs, sign up for their newsletters, watch them present, examine the content they create, and track how they sell.

What are they doing well? What have they stopped doing? How are they executing their ideas? How can you model some of those ideas?

Dig deep. Analyze their actions. Print out samples of the content they create. Watch the response of their base. Take note of the kind of results they achieve. Apply some of their best ideas to your business.

Here are a few ways to find role models:

Ask other people: Ask your peers and other industry experts who their role models are, and why. You'll assemble a nice list of possibilities. Remember, they don't need to be in your industry.

Look for experts: Every industry has them. Closely examine why others classify these people as experts. Take a look at what they create and determine if any of them would be a good role model for your business.

Look to big brands: Whether you're a one-person operation or a Fortune 100 company, looking to well-known brands can be a good source of inspiration.

AN UNLIKELY ROLE MODEL EXAMPLE

Consider the restaurant chain Panera Bread, a billion-dollar bakery/café that specializes in bagels, breads, sandwiches, soups, and salads.

Ron Shaich is the CEO and co-founder. He differentiated his company among the fast-food industry by focusing on healthy alternatives.

If you've been in a Panera restaurant, you know they allocate an enormous amount of space to their seating area. They were among the first fast-food restaurants to offer free wireless Web access to customers. A significant portion of their display space is dedicated to showcasing their dessert bakeries.

So what can Panera Bread teach you if you're not in the restaurant business? How could this company become a role model for yours?

Walk into a Panera Bread restaurant and take a close look at the experience others are having. One of the first things you'll likely notice is that businesspeople go there to get work done. You might see men and women with laptops and paperwork. While speaking to the manager at my local Panera Bread, he told me it's not unusual for some customers to spend eight hours there!

You also might notice the free samples of bread the moment you walk through the door. Or maybe the loyalty program for frequent customers. Perhaps the changing menu items will catch your eye.

You might come to the conclusion that for Panera customers, good food in a comfortable environment is more important than price. What likely brings people back again is the overall experience.

How can you create an experience for your business that brings people back again and again—whether you have a physical or online presence? Should you provide a free sample of something? If you did, might it get customers to try something new?

"If you're really smart, there's no one you don't learn from. It's not copying. It's learning from experience. And lots of people have learned from Panera," Shaich told a *USA Today* reporter.[2]

This example demonstrates how an unlikely source can serve as a role model. If you watch for them, you'll begin to see all sorts of possible business role models.

Once you've identified a few role models, *study them*. Take some of their best ideas and test them out with your business. Don't stop tracking your role models. When you see them change, take note.

Back when I was in college, I worked for Sears, selling televisions. When I walked past the guy selling rugs—a wise older man—I'd always ask him how he was doing. He often responded, "The biggest room in my house is the room for improvement." That was memorable wisdom from a carpet salesman. It's also a wise mentality to apply to your business. A good role model will inspire you to improve.

Role models can also fall into the category of "other people" described in the elevation principle. A role model today could become a strategic partner tomorrow. For example, Andrew Goodman went on to write for one of my publications, and later helped me promote some of my services.

The right role models will inspire you to take your rocket ship to new places. Diligently seek them out.

Not only can people and businesses serve as role models, so can content.

Leveraging Inspirational Content

Have you ever been wowed by something you've seen from another business? Maybe it was a brilliantly crafted article or a well-produced video.

---

[2] Horovitz, B. "Panera Bakes a Recipe for Success," *USA Today,* July 23, 2009. www .usatoday.com/money/industries/food/2009-07-22-panera-success-different-strategy_ N.htm.

These types of content are inspiration pieces. Unique from role models, content of this sort can be produced by anyone. Thus, you might find inspirational pieces during random Internet surfs.

Inspirational content is a rare find. It serves as an example to strive toward with your own creations.

You can gain amazing creative insight from great works of written content, well-produced videos, and audio broadcasts. These categories of content can also help stir your creative juices when you're feeling stale.

WHY INSPIRATIONAL CONTENT?

Remember, the first element of the elevation principle is great content. It's what will fuel your business. You'll need to create it to achieve business growth. Although in later chapters I will show you how to create content, you'll need ongoing inspiration to keep producing great content.

When you find inspirational content, you'll know it. It will connect with you on multiple levels. It will engage you.

Inspirational content helps you by providing a model you can strive to emulate. That model might include a unique writing style, creative layout, an innovative use of story, or stunning imagery.

Here's an example:

In 2006 I happened across a terrific ebook by Brian Clark called *Viral Copy*.[3] It was a brilliant piece about the type of content that resonates with and is shared by people.

But what struck me the most about the 30-page document was the way Brian wrote it. He used short sentences. His language was informal, and there was no pitch.

Viral Copy not only became a valuable resource for me as a new blogger, it also became an inspiration for me when creating similar content. I referenced it frequently.

Here's a second example:

In the previous chapter I mentioned how I followed an Internet guru who ultimately produced gravity drag for my business.

Even though I was repulsed by my experience with this guy's program, I did gain a few good ideas that were worth modeling.

---

[3] See http://downloads.copyblogger.com/Viral_Copy.pdf.

For example, I recalled seeing a video he had produced. It was a behind-the-scenes type of video, in which he spoke and shared stories while he was going from one scene to the next. The whole time he was talking to the camera as if he were talking to me, personally. It was as if I were walking beside him while he spoke.

I took that great content idea and began producing regular videos of me walking in different locations and talking directly to the camera. I called them my "walking man" videos.

One of my videos took place while I was driving my car to my office, and ultimately took the viewer into my building, down the hall, through the front door of my office, and right to my desk. Another one occurred while I was walking past a waterfront shopping center.

These videos resonated with people. Had I not initially made a note of that inspiration video, I might have never thought of modeling it for my content creation.

Having inspirational content readily available can be a big challenge, however. So you'll need a system to help you store and easily access your valuable discoveries.

Setting Up an Idea Vault

Are you so busy with your daily responsibilities that you have little time for creative thinking? If so, you're not alone.

Ideas are treasures we want but rarely seek. And when it comes to developing great content, you'll need ideas.

Where do fresh ideas come from?

"Ideas don't need a passport, and often cross borders (of all kinds) with impunity," explained Seth Godin.[4]

Ideas are out there, right in front of you. As your rocket ship propels through space, you'll find great ideas. You simply need to grab and store them.

There's a time and a place to execute great ideas. Likely, however, it's not when you first discover them. And be forewarned: When ideas come your way they won't stay for long. The worries of your work will repel them—sometimes forever.

---

[4] Godin, S. *Seth's Blog,* "Where Do Ideas Come From?," November 24, 2010.

That's why you need an *idea vault*—a place where your ideas can live and be easily fetched when needed.

When I was in college, I often flew home to my family during holiday breaks. While stuck at 40,000 feet above the United States, I'd read those airline magazines tucked in the seatback in front of me.

Whenever I found something interesting or really creative, I simply ripped out the pages. Everything ended up in a manila file folder for possible later use.

Some of those ideas remain in the folder to this very day. Others I referenced years after I discovered them. But one thing's for sure: Those ideas haven't gone anywhere.

You may not read as many magazines as you used to. But ideas are still out there. They're on your favorite Web sites, in e-mail attachments, and in your physical mailbox.

You're seeing them. Now start capturing them.

Here are a few ways to capture ideas:

♦ *Bookmark services:* You could simply use a bookmark service like Delicious.com to file and tag your online discoveries with relevant keywords like "inspiration," and "content." This becomes a collection of links to other Web pages.

♦ *Store them in e-mail:* Try setting up a special folder using your e-mail application. Then simply send yourself an e-mail with links or attachments (like white papers) that you want to file for later access. You'll be able to easily search them later.

♦ *Store on your desktop:* Why not create a folder on your desktop labeled "Ideas"? Then make PDF versions of your favorite articles and begin storing them. Sometimes links expire, so it's wise to maintain your own electronic copies.

♦ *Set up physical files:* Having a physical idea vault is often a good idea. Not only can you print out great content, but you can also store ideas you read in print or that arrive by mail.

Idea vaults are easy to create. Start one today. Reference what you find tomorrow, or the day after.

An idea vault does you no good, however, if you don't find great content. You'll need a robust discovery system to find inspirational content.

Creating a Discovery System

Finding inspirational content will be essential for keeping your ideas fresh. Putting the right systems in place will help you easily find what you're seeking.

A discovery system is a simple set of steps you perform regularly to ensure you find the *best content and people* in your industry. It involves watching to see what and who are popular, trending, or influential.

As your rocket ship journeys through the cosmos, your discovery systems will ensure you are on the edge of content innovation.

For example, someone on my team monitors a number of Web sites in my space for hot news, interesting articles, and research studies.

Each day we take two of the best links and feed them to our reader base via numerous social media channels. We track how people respond to our updates and use that as a gauge to determine possible topics for future articles.

Here are some of the benefits of a robust discovery system:

◆ *You'll find influential people:* A major advantage of a discovery system is it can help you identify other people (the second part of the elevation principle) who are influential in your industry.
◆ *You'll know what to create:* By monitoring all the critical Web sites in your industry, you'll be able to quickly and easily see what content is popular. If you see a new idea, topic, or angle that you haven't covered, capture it. It could provide ideas for your content creation efforts or your idea vault.
◆ *You'll identify industry trends:* Such a system also keeps you informed on the latest happenings in your industry. You'll be able to easily identify trends that can help you plan for the future.
◆ *You'll find content to share:* Sharing great content from other people should be part of your model. With a good discovery system in place, you'll easily find new and popular content to share.

HOW TO DISCOVER CONTENT

What follows are some ideas to get you started:

Bookmark Folders   The Safari browser (from Apple) and Firefox browser both have a cool feature called bookmark folders. With folders, you can group many bookmarks into a folder. In Safari you can display that folder as a tiny little button that lives in the bookmarks bar. When you click that button, up pops all the different Web sites simultaneously—each assigned its own tab. In Firefox, the folder can also live in the Bookmarks bar. To open all Web sites simultaneously in different tabs, you select the option at the bottom of your bookmarks list.

Thus you could find five or six Web sites that are regularly producing content that you think is interesting in your industry. Then you could set up a bookmark folder containing links to all the sites. When you push the button, instantly all the content from all the different pages comes up, each in a unique tab.

You can peruse them literally in seconds, to see the latest topics that sites are writing about. That's how you can discover new ideas to talk about.

For example, I have a bookmark folder set up for social media news. It goes to 11 different Web sites instantly. Very quickly I can keep up with my industry, discover great content to share, and find inspirational pieces for my idea vault.

Google News   The site news.google.com aggregates news from thousands of sources into a single searchable site. If you were tracking Facebook, for example, you could easily search for all the latest news on that topic.

After you do a few different keyword searches, you could simply bookmark the pages and add them to your bookmarks folder. Alternatively, you could add your search result to an RSS (Really Simple Syndication) reader.

Google Alerts   With this service, Google can e-mail you a daily digest of all the critical articles occurring around a search phrase. Google peruses online publications and blogs, and then sends you just the top couple relevant links.

Guzzle.it   This is one of the coolest sites I've come across for discovering new content. When you go to this Web site, all you have to do is put in some keywords and it creates special feeds for you. This Web site scans hundreds of major publications and social bookmarking sites, finding the hot content that people are talking about. You can set this up for any set of keywords that you want.

Search.Twitter.com The search function in Twitter allows you to easily discover the most popular content on Twitter in the last day or two. For example, if you cover the marketing world, you could simply type "marketing" in the search field. The most commonly shared tweets will be at the top of the page, along with the author and how long ago they were tweeted.

Delicious.com This social bookmarking site is the place to go for rich content that people want to come back to. Where Twitter is focused on hot new content, with Delicious you'll be able to find new and timeless content. All you need to do is type in a keyword phrase and you'll see links to articles, along with the number of people who have bookmarked them.

You'll even see a timeline trend that tracks bookmarked content for your keyword search over time. This can be helpful to determine whether your topic is a rising or declining topic on Delicious. For example, bookmarks on the phrase "white papers" peaked in February of 2007 and have been in steady decline since then. In contrast, bookmarks about Facebook began a major upward spike around the same time period.

■ ■ ■

These resources are a mere sampling of the possibilities available. Your goal should be to select a few and set them into a regular pattern of activity.

You'll also want to discover important people.

How to Discover People

Discovering content is only the first half of a discovery system. You'll also need systems in place to discover *other people*—the second critical component of the elevation principle. While content fuels your rocket ship, other people move it to new places.

There are many reasons you'll want to discover other people. Other people could serve as role models for your business. You'll also want to produce content that focuses on the successful efforts of others—something your base will find valuable. Additionally, some of those other people could turn out to become fire starters for you.

Ask People You Trust David Garland from TheRiseToTheTop.com regularly interviews successful entrepreneurs for his online show. I asked him how he finds people for his video blog. He explained that people he trusts introduce him to experts. Those trusted sources also suggest that the expert be on David's show.

He said, "It started as me asking people I knew and has grown since then, where it is much more inbound than outbound. I try to be more selective now than at the beginning, when I was getting going. Now I try for the very best unique, passionate, interesting entrepreneurs and creative people."

When David asked me to be on his show, he handled it entirely through someone I know and respect. Because of the trust I had in this mutual friend, I was confident that being on David's show—which I was then unfamiliar with—would be a worthwhile experience.

Amazon's Hot New Releases List If you want to find up-and-coming stars, here's a little-known secret: Amazon has an upcoming bestsellers list. These are not necessarily bestsellers yet. What they are are books that will be coming out in the future or were just released.

Amazon ranks the books into hundreds of different categories and subgroups. Here's an example: Business & Investing → Marketing & Sales → Consumer Behavior. Then it classifies books by presales numbers. It will show you all the new books that are coming out and it will tell you the authors of those books.

What do you do with that? You *contact those authors* and say, "Hey, I'd love to interview you and talk about your new book." This is a great way for you to plant a little equity inside the accounts of these up-and-coming authors before they get huge. You'll also be able to get direct access to already successful authors who have new books coming out.

These authors are *hungry* to speak about their topic when they've got a new book coming out. Often, they'll accept any kind of press. And this means they're going to be more than willing to talk with you.

You can take a look at the master list here: www.amazon.com/gp/new-releases/books. You'll see all the master categories on the left side of the page. Just pick a category and start digging deeper.

Conferences   Even if you don't attend the popular events in your industry, there's nothing wrong with scouting the speaker's list for potential experts. Oftentimes event organizers select presenters based on their likelihood to lure attendees. *Speakers are typically very open to speaking to others about their topical expertise.*

When I attend big events, like BlogWorld, we carefully look over the entire list of speakers and handpick people we'd like to interview. Some of those interviews are done by phone and transcribed into articles. However, we like doing on-camera interviews with experts. For example, at BlogWorld 2010, we captured 29 interviews that we released over many months on SocialMediaExaminer.com. Some of the folks we interviewed we later asked to present at our own events.

■ ■ ■

The preceding list is just a sampling of how to discover other people that you might want to interview for future content. Setting up a discovery system for people also helps you find possible role models and set future potential relationships in motion.

Why the Outward Focus?

This chapter focused on role models, inspirational content, idea vaults, and discovery systems. At their core, all of these concepts involve looking outside the walls of your typical thinking.

I could have easily not included this chapter and simply remained focused on vision, goals, and trajectory. However, I believe, from firsthand experience, that it's too easy to become myopic and self-focused. This shortsightedness is precisely why so many businesses experience gravity drag.

Like space, your industry is in constant motion. To stay on course, you *need to look outside your rocket ship window*—always watching for inspiration.

By finding role models—whether people or businesses—you'll be inspired to reach further and try new ideas. You'll also discover people who could become important future strategic partners for your business.

Remember, it's other people who move your ship to new places. Identifying great people who can serve as role models and possible future fire starters can encourage you to think bigger.

Content is what fuels your rocket. A key part of your mission will involve discovering great new content during your journey. With your discoveries, you'll be motivated to improve your own content and try new ideas. You'll also need ample cargo holds for your discoveries—and that's where your idea vault comes in.

Commit to looking outside. Take a cue from the U.S. space program. Don't let the Sputniks of your industry stop you from creating amazing content and forging strong relationships with others.

■ ■ ■

This chapter examined the importance of looking outward to other people and their content. It revealed how to find role models and inspirational material. It took a close look at how to store ideas for later use (before they disappear forever). The chapter also demonstrated how to set up discovery systems that help you find great content and people.

You should now have all of the core elements of your mission plan mapped out: Your vision, goals, and trajectory should be clear. You should have markers established that help you move between your goals. Your role models should be identified, along with the systems to capture and store ideas and content.

The next chapter will focus on mastering a core element of the elevation principle: working with other people.

Leveraging the Power of Other People

I am the people—the mob—the crowd—the mass. Do you know that all the great work of the world is done through me?

—Carl Sandburg, 1950

People built Rome. People put a man on the moon. And it will be other people who take your business to outer space and beyond.

In 1948, Dick and Mac McDonald opened the first McDonald's self-service drive-in restaurant. They designed a system to rapidly deliver a simple menu of burgers, fries, shakes, soft drinks, and apple pies to guests.

Ray Kroc—a milkshake machine salesman—visited a McDonald's restaurant in 1955. He was impressed, and suggested McDonald's consider starting a franchise. Kroc offered to take on the burden for the unconvinced McDonald brothers. They agreed.

By 1959, 101 McDonald's restaurants had sold more than 100 million hamburgers. In 1961, Kroc bought out the McDonald brothers and went on to lead a massive expansion of the company.

As this story demonstrates, other people can help take your business to unimaginable places. They are also a critical element of the elevation principle. Other people determine where your rocket ship goes, and how quickly. The key to activating the power of other people is to do great things for them—*without expecting anything in return.*

This chapter will examine three types of other people who are essential to your business growth: your *reader base, outside experts,* and *fire starters.*

The Power of Other People

In the context of marketing, the power brokers used to be the people who controlled the traditional media. *Now the people with enormous influence are everyday people, like you and me.*

This power shift is due to the mass adoption of social media.

"Social media has altered the scale and velocity of word of mouth," explained David Jones, CEO of the 12,000-employee ad agency Havas Worldwide. "For example, we did the Roller Babies ad for Evian. This was the most downloaded piece of commercial content in history, with 125 million YouTube downloads. *Time* named it the TV ad of the year in 2009, yet it had never been on TV."[1]

Social media has fundamentally altered the way people share. "Now we've got this big tool to take word of mouth that might have been one-to-one or one-to-two, and suddenly it's one-to-1,000 or one-to-50,000," explained Andy Sernovitz, author, *Word of Mouth Marketing* (Kaplan Business, 2006).[2]

This meteoric shift is equivalent to the invention of the automobile. With the invention of cars, people were able to expand their known world. With the massive growth of social media, anyone anywhere can group together and have a massive impact.

With the click of a button, people can share your great content with all of their friends and fans. For your business this represents an incredible opportunity to be quickly discovered—without reliance on traditional costly marketing methods.

---

[1] Cited in Flamm, M. Movers & Shakers: "Old-media pro on succeeding in new world," *Crain's New York Business,* November 21, 2010. www.crainsnewyork.com/article/20101121/SUB/311219993.

[2] Stelzner, M. "How Big Brands Employ Social Media Marketing," August 26, 2010, Social Media Examiner, www.socialmediaexaminer.com/interview-andy-sernovitz/.

When you build a strong base of readers, they become a powerful force that can propel your rocket ship. People consume the fuel (your great content) taking your rocket ship sky-high very quickly. Your goal is to resonate with the right people.

Who Do You Want to Reach?

Ray Kroc knew he wanted to reach on-the-go families living in suburban neighborhoods. Whom do you want to reach?

You'll need to attract a base of people on whom you can build your business. They're the people you'll create content for. They're the force that moves your rocket ship forward.

The people in your base usually comprise readers of your blog, subscribers to your content, fans of your social media sites, and your customers.

Your goal should be to *come up with a specific and detailed profile of the people you want to reach*, making it easier to create great content for them and to find relevant experts.

When determining the profile of these people, you'll want to be targeted and precise. The broader your audience, the harder it will be for you to connect with them.

David Meerman Scott, in his book *The New Rules of Marketing and PR: How to Use News Releases, Blogs, Podcasting, Viral Marketing, and Online Media to Reach Buyers Directly* (Wiley, 2007), introduced the concept of *buyer personas*. He explains that if you can classify buyers (or readers) into a distinct group, and document what you know about them, you can easily create targeted content for that group. Scott adds that the interests, problems, and desires of various persona groups should be carefully examined and written down.

He says, "By truly understanding the market problems that your products and services solve for your buyer personas, you transform your marketing from mere product-specific, egocentric gobbledygook that only you understand and care about, into valuable information people are eager to consume."[3] And when people eagerly consume your fuel, your business will quickly grow.

---

[3] Scott, D.M. "How well do you know your buyer personas?," *WebInkNow blog*, March 23, 2008. www.webinknow.com/2008/07/how-well-do-you.html.

In context of the elevation principle, buyer personas might be better classified as people personas. *The end game is to attract many people, only a portion of whom will become future customers.* By broadening the term from *buyer* to *people,* you'll have room to attract future evangelists who may never purchase from you, but who will happily spread the word about your great content, driving more people to your business.

PERSONA EXAMPLES

Internet software company HubSpot (which I introduced in Chapter 1) has two primary personas: Owner Ollie and Marketer Mary.[4]

Owner Ollie is a small business owner with fewer than 25 employees. Ollie is busy managing human resources, marketing, sales, operations, and finance for his company, and has little time left for executing new ideas. He lacks on-staff marketing resources and does most of his company's marketing himself. He's curious about inbound marketing, but hasn't made any significant investments. His top priority is generating new leads for his business.

Marketer Mary works as a marketer for a small business, with 26 to 100 employees. A marketing team supports Mary and the programs she oversees. She is familiar with newer inbound marketing techniques and is actively seeking help with running, evaluating, and justifying her marketing investments to upper management. Mary wants sophisticated measurement tools, and has money to spend on her marketing programs.

As you can see from these two examples, HubSpot has two very clear groups it targets with its content.

"Our content strategy for us really boils down to who the persona is that we're trying to reach. We're trying to reach small business owners and marketing professionals at small- and medium-size businesses. We think about: What is the content that's interesting to them and what's going to be useful and valuable to them? Then that's the content we try to produce," explained Mike Volpe, HubSpot's vice president of marketing.

---

[4] Steenburgh, T., Avery, J. & Dahod, N. "HubSpot: Inbound marketing and Web 2.0," *Harvard Business Review,* May 28, 2009. hbr.org/product/hubspot-inbound-marketing-and-web-2-0/an/509049-PDF-ENG.

Notice that Volpe didn't say, "And then we try to sell to them." Rather, he said HubSpot creates content that is useful and valuable to the company's base.

Who do you want to reach? Is there some group of people that you'd love to get in front of? Building a profile (or persona) for your ideal people base is an essential first step toward reaching them.

Developing Profiles for Your Ideal Reader Base

You can likely describe the primary buyer of your products and services without batting an eye. Now I'd like you to take it a bit further. Don't think about people as targets for the sale. The question isn't who can you land, it's who can you help?

Rather than focus on people who are buying your products and services, shift your attention to people you want to help—regardless of whether they purchase or not. Your objective should be to focus on who you want reading your blog, subscribing to your content, and becoming fans of your social media sites.

Why? The power of people goes way beyond the sale. Among your base, some people will purchase your wares, others will evangelize your content, and still others will contribute to your community. If you're only focused on the sale, you're missing a mega opportunity.

WHO SHOULD YOU TARGET?

Let's say your company makes software products that help coders. You've got a decent-size customer base of techie folks who love your products.

However, every time you try to sell to new prospects, you must convince the coder's boss that investing in your expensive solution is a smart move for the company. Who should you focus on for your ideal base: the coder or the coder's boss?

If your reader base is full of coder bosses and you continually provide highly valuable content to those bosses, you'll have access directly to the very people you've been struggling to convince.

If these bosses are already familiar with your great content, there's no question that your path to these influential people will be easy to travel. The thought process for the boss might be something like this:

"I'm familiar with the great content these guys provide for free. Maybe I should consider looking at their application."

In the end, you'll sell more products (and more quickly) because you've captured the eyes and minds of the people making the decisions. And those techies who love you will grow as a consequence.

Decide precisely who you want to target and then dig deeper. What follows are some ways you can refine your ideal base. Consider taking some notes as you proceed.

IDEAL INDUSTRY

Determine if it makes sense for you to focus on an industry when developing a profile for your reader base.

A significant 82 percent of businesspeople find content that is specific to their industry most valuable, according to a study by MarketingSherpa.[5]

For example, rather than targeting chief marketing officers (CMOs) across all industries, you might want to consider CMOs in a specific vertical industry. CMOs in the automotive industry face a different set of challenges than their peers in the pet food or enterprise software industries.

WhitePaperSource.com focuses on two different industries: business-to-business software companies and the freelance writing space. Its newsletter provides a mix of content that appeals to these two different groups. Software companies are the businesses most likely to produce white papers. Freelancers are most interested in determining how to create white papers and pitch themselves as guns for hire to the software companies.

Determine if there's an industry or two that you should focus on. If there are, write them down now. Continue to refine the profile of your ideal base using the criteria in the following sections.

TOPICAL INTERESTS

Sometimes it makes sense to focus on a topic your reader base is very interested in. If you decide to go down this road, make sure the topic

---

[5] MarketingSherpa. "2009–2008 Business Technology Marketing Benchmark Guide," 2009. www.marketingsherpa.com/page/marketing_plan?9896#btbmg.

has longevity or that you have the flexibility to change the topical focus.

You can examine a topic within a specific industry or a topic that transcends all industries.

SocialMediaExaminer.com has as its topical focus social media, with an emphasis on marketing and customer support. When I started the site, I saw the enormity of social media and knew my addressable market was all businesses of all sizes in all parts of the world. It is rare that a single topic can have enough sustaining power to transcend industries.

At the same time, I was fully aware that the buzz and longevity of the topic of social media would likely have a shelf life of three to five years from the moment the site launched.

Topics can also be overly broad and thus fail to appeal to any particular base. For example, had I decided to focus just on marketing, we would not have achieved the kind of traction we did with Social MediaExaminer.com.

Are there a few topics your ideal base is highly interested in? Add them to your developing profile.

JOB TITLE AND FUNCTION

The MarketingSherpa study I mentioned a few paragraphs earlier also examined the impact of job-function-focused content. A significant 64 percent of businesspeople find content focused on their work roles to be engaging.

Try to determine the most likely job title or role for the people in your reader base. Are they stay-at-home moms, salespeople, finance directors, or small business owners? Try to come up with a specific list of job functions for these people.

For SocialMediaExaminer.com, the job roles of our readers are primarily marketing professionals and small business owners. In both cases, these individuals are responsible for finding leads, increasing sales, and generating greater awareness for their businesses.

Start brainstorming the job titles and functions of your ideal base. You'll probably come up with a bunch of ideas. Then try to narrow your list down to one or two very specific job titles.

Keep going back to the word "ideal" in your mind. Rather than thinking, "Anybody who's a director of any division." Ask yourself which kind of director is more ideal?

Once you've determined the job title, think about the duties of someone in that role. Are there specific tasks he or she performs and that can drive your content strategy?

Write down the typical job titles and functions of people in your ideal reader base.

COMPANY SIZE

How big is the business you're targeting? Do you want readers who work at *Fortune 500* companies or midsized businesses, or are you targeting the self-employed?

If your target is a consumer, skip forward to the next section.

What quantifier of size are you looking at? Are you measuring the number of employees, sales figures, or number of physical attributes (like hospital beds, storefronts, or hotel rooms)?

If you're thinking of targeting a big company, you'll want to dig a little bit deeper. What does "big" mean to you? For one business, a big company might be 1,000 employees, and for another it might be 100,000 employees.

When you document the size of a company, try to quantify its size to help you understand and distinguish it from other companies.

GEOGRAPHY

Should you focus on people in specific locations? Does your reader base live mostly in Latin America? Are you targeting people in the United States? Maybe they're in your local community?

Is there anything unique about the place where your base lives and works that you should take into consideration? Do the people in this part of the world have cultural nuances or unique interests?

For example, *The Pioneer Woman* blog caters to women living in the rural countrysides of America. Its author, Ree Drummond, married a cowboy and moved out of the big city. Her blog embraces the rural culture.

Add any geographical considerations to your developing profile of your ideal base.

You can see that by examining industry, topic, job function, company size, and geography, you'll be able to draw a clearer picture of your reader base.

If you targeted your content to a specific industry, a specific job function, and a specific-size company, how much more would your content resonate with people? How would people react as they consumed your fuel?

If you further narrowed your base using a shared topical interest within a physical location, would the makeup of your reader base become even clearer?

The more refined your reader base is, the more targeted your content can become, and, thus, the better it will resonate with people. And when people find value in your content, they'll send your rocket ship higher.

How to Identify the Problems and Desires of Your Reader Base

Once you have a general understanding of the who, what, and where of your ideal reader base, it's important to focus on their challenges, attitudes, knowledge, and desires.

Going further than a general profile will help you craft content that deeply resonates with people. Developing a more intimate knowledge of your base will separate you from your competitors.

If you can connect with people at an emotional level, they'll feel more closely connected to your rocket ship. The result? They'll gladly help your business grow.

The following sections contain questions you'll want to answer.

What Problems Are They Facing?

When you understand the core challenges faced by your reader base, you can easily draw people to your company simply by helping them solve their problems.

For example, when I started SocialMediaExaminer.com, I knew that marketers were struggling to figure out how to use the non-intuitive social media tools of the day. I also knew that the constant innovation among social media sites made it hard for people to keep up with the changes.

Armed with this knowledge, I developed content that met the immediate needs of my base.

What problems is your reader base facing? Can you help them solve some of their issues?

By the way, if you're not sure what your readers' problems are, why not simply ask them? A simple survey can go a long way toward rounding out a great profile.

Go back to your description of your base and write down a list of their problems.

WHAT'S THE NATURE OF THE PEOPLE I WANT TO REACH?

This is a very important question to ask. Are these people very busy? Are they actively seeking new ideas?

If they're busy, you're going to have to get to the point rapidly with your content—and you're going to have to respect their lack of time. If they're actively seeking new ideas, it means your reader base is going to want richer content.

Here's another question you might want to ask: "Are these people naturally skeptical?" If your base is full of skeptics, you're going to need to try to provide more evidence in your content. Skeptics need proof. This means you may want to share case studies of others achieving success as part of your content model.

Are you dealing with a crowd full of know-it-alls? In this case, you'll need to make sure your content goes deeper than information your readers typically find elsewhere. Highly knowledgeable people often aren't seeking new knowledge. However, if you offer up new ideas they've never seen before, you'll quickly become a trusted resource for them.

If you're not sure what the general nature of your base is, start talking to people who are just like your ideal readers. Ask how busy they are, and whether research is a part of their daily tasks. Then ask whether they are generally open to change.

Document some of the attitudes and dispositions of your reader base.

HOW FAMILIAR ARE THEY WITH MY TOPIC?

This is an important consideration that's often overlooked. How much does your reader base already know about the topics you'll be focusing on?

In the case of SocialMediaExaminer.com, I knew when we began that most of our readers would be new to the "how" of social media marketing. That dictated the type of content we created. For example, one of our more popular articles was titled, "Facebook 101 for Business: Your Complete Guide," crafted by Mari Smith (co-author of the book, with Chris Treadaway, of *Facebook Marketing: An Hour a Day*; Sybex, 2010).

However, we also knew that a significant portion of our audience was comprised of very knowledgeable social media practitioners. So our content strategy included a fair amount of more advanced topics, to keep that subset of our base coming back to our site.

Ask yourself: "On a scale of 1 to 10, where does my reader base's topical knowledge land?" A complete newbie would be a 1 and a highly knowledgeable expert a 10. This will help you test your content ideas against the insights of your base.

Knowing the knowledge level of your readers also helps you decide whether you should carefully define important terms, or if doing so would be an insult to them.

Identify the familiarity level of your reader base with the types of topics you'll be writing about, and add that to their profile description.

WHAT ARE THE DESIRES OF MY READER BASE?

What does your reader base really want?

"Universal motivations and desires are symbols that are hot-branded into our psyches. They work in tandem with our emotions. They shape who we are and what roles we play," said Barry Feig in his book *Hot Button Marketing*.[6]

Feig opens his book by sharing a story about George Eastman, the founder of Kodak. Eastman asked some of his employees, "What are we selling?" Many said cameras.

Eastman explained they were wrong. Cameras were simply a by-product of what they were really selling—memories. He explained that people don't want cameras, they want lasting memories.

---

[6] Feig, B. "Hot Button Marketing: Push the Emotional Buttons That Get People to Buy," Adams Media, 2006.

Armed with that knowledge, you now understand why Kodak places "Kodak Moments" signs in strategic locations at major theme parks.

By identifying the desires of your base, you can attempt to satisfy their needs at an emotional level. Feig explains that if you win their hearts, their minds will follow.

Here are some of the more common desires identified by Feig:

◆ Control
◆ Superiority
◆ Discovery
◆ Family values
◆ Belonging
◆ Fun
◆ More time
◆ Only the best
◆ Self-achievement
◆ Helping others
◆ Reinventing oneself

This list is just a sampling of the 16 desires outlined in Feig's outstanding book.

Ask yourself whether your reader base has strong desires in any of these categories. For example, if you're targeting stay-at-home moms, you might determine that they desire more time, helping others, family values, discovery, and fun. With this knowledge you could produce content that helps them meet some of their desires.

Add a list of your ideal base's desires to your profile. If you are similar to the people in your reader base, ask yourself what you desire.

Visualize Your Reader Base

Now stop here: *Spend some quality time studying, thinking, and profiling your reader base.* Your goal should be to produce a single paragraph that describes your ideal base with crystal clarity.

By understanding precisely who you're trying to reach, you'll be far ahead of your competitors and know precisely whom you need to help—and what type of content you'll need to do so. A clear profile also helps you say no when you're tempted to travel to an off-the-map destination in pursuit of something irrelevant to your readers.

Your end result should be a profile that others can easily understand (such as the Marketer Mary example from HubSpot).

Sometimes you can even visualize an actual person who matches your ideal base profile. David Meerman Scott explained how the company Kadient has two life-sized cutouts of its profiles, named Anya and Luke.[7] These serve as physical reminders for the company's marketing team.

You don't need cutouts, but you do need a very clear understanding of the people who make up your reader base.

Remember the power of people. They'll take your rocket ship high and far if you give them what they want. To do that, you must know them well. In later chapters I will show you how to create content for these people.

Your base is the first of three people groups you'll want to focus on. The next group is experts outside of your company.

Working with Outside Experts

Experts are the people your reader base turns to when they need advice or insight. They're trusted because of their deep experience, training, and knowledge.

Working with experts outside the walls of your business is one of the least-utilized yet most powerful ways to grow your business. Experts bring credibility, experience, and exposure to your business.

Working with experts is like taking your rocket ship through a wormhole. They have what your readers seek—important, worthwhile knowledge. And some experts have a large following of their own. These factors often combine, creating a shortcut that can put you far ahead of your competition.

Getting experts involved is much easier than it seems.

If you know your reader base well, finding experts who can help them overcome their challenges (or meet their desires) has a powerful

---

[7] Scott, D.M. "How well do you know your buyer personas?," *Web Ink Now Blog,* July 22, 2008.

effect. There are many ways experts can aid in your content creation, which I'll show you in the following sections.

Perhaps you're wondering why you need to work with experts outside your business. Why would they have any desire to work with you?

Maybe you're an expert already? Or perhaps you're a total newbie and intimidated by the thought of working with experts? Let me address each of these with a story.

WORKING WITH OTHERS WHEN YOU ARE THE EXPERT

Even if you are considered an expert in your industry (or you have experts within your company), it's good to embrace people from the outside, for a couple of reasons. For one, seeking and sharing opinions from your peers and other experts *eliminates the perception of self-serving bias*. It also *provides a source of great content* for your reader base.

Prior to publishing my first book, *Writing White Papers: How to Capture Readers and Keep Them Engaged* (WhitePaperSource Publishing, 2006), I identified a handful of other thought leaders who specialized in creating white papers. Gordon Graham and Jonathan Kantor were two people I knew who were already producing great content.

I was their direct competitor.

Nevertheless, I reached out to them by phone and asked if they'd be willing to publish some of their thoughts on white papers to my growing newsletter list. I explained that they'd get profitable exposure for their businesses. They both agreed to participate.

My audience was thrilled to hear from other experts. Jonathan and Gordon didn't always agree with me, but they added a rich perspective to my reader base. Sometimes, I would write about them in my articles. Other times, they would write original pieces for my newsletter. Eventually, they became regular contributors and, later, strategic partners.

My attitude all along was that we were building something bigger than our individual businesses. We were evangelizing the world on the value of white paper marketing. As a result, the acceptance of white paper marketing was rising—and taking Gordon and Jonathan's rocket ships up with it. I called what we were doing *coopitition*, a contraction of *cooperation* and *competition*.

These two experts helped me take my rocket ship to unimaginable heights. They also benefited greatly as a result, winning new business and being associated as regular contributors to what we built.

Keep in mind that, all along, *there was no question that I owned my rocket ship and that they were contributing.* That said, I made sure they received meaningful value from the relationship—so much so that they would never question my control of my own ship.

For example, I often invited them to speak on panels with me, and promoted them as two of the top three white paper writers in the world. A key to working with other experts is making sure they're gaining enough value in the relationship that they want to continue.

When you're an expert, working with outsiders helps *establish greater credibility for your content, provides a platform for your peers, and helps you grow quickly.*

On the flip side, what if you're not an expert? How could working with experts help your business?

WORKING WITH EXPERTS WHEN YOU'RE NOT ONE

In the white paper world, I was an expert. In the social media world, I was nowhere close to an expert. In fact, I was a behind-the-times newbie in every way. I had been experimenting with social media for only about nine months before I started SocialMediaExaminer.com.

I knew when I started the site I'd be highly reliant on outside experts. So I handpicked a short list of specialists I knew, and who knew me.

They included names like Jason Falls, Denise Wakeman, Chris Garrett, and Mari Smith. Each of these people had demonstrated expertise in unique areas related to social media. They weren't just experts, though; they could also write.

I explained the need in the marketplace for an online magazine that offered rich content. In each case I explained how participating would benefit their personal brands and businesses.

I asked them each if they'd be willing to contribute one article a month to my new site. They knew my track record, bought into my vision, and agreed to contribute original content.

But I didn't stop there. I also asked them to identify other top experts. As I traveled to trade shows, I made a point of interviewing these experts, often on camera. Those I couldn't land on camera I interviewed by phone. As a social media newbie (very similar to my ideal base), I knew what questions to ask.

After only a few months I had an enormous amount of quality content coming in from Jason Falls and company. I also had lots of compelling and thought-provoking videos from my interviews with experts like Chris Brogan and Frank Eliason.

I started recruiting some of the experts from my video interviews to pen articles for our site. When they saw that their respected peers were already doing so, their decision was very easy.

For SocialMediaExaminer.com, outside experts became not only a source of great content for my reader base, they also helped spread the word about our site, delivering a lot of traffic.

I know that the site wouldn't have become as popular as it did without the help of outside experts.

■ ■ ■

As these two stories demonstrate, the power of working with experts outside your company can be enormous. Experts can take your rocket ship quickly to places you'd never be able to reach on your own.

What Outside Experts Can Do for You

Embracing authorities outside of your business can have a massive impact on the movement of your rocket ship.

Here are some of the many benefits of working with outside experts:

- *Provides a rich source of content:* Experts are full of amazing content. You can mine their knowledge via interviews or by recruiting them to create content for you.
- *Grows your reader base:* When experts share knowledge that meets the needs and desires of your reader base, they will be hooked, and share your content with their peers. The notoriety of experts will also draw more people to your site. Some experts will share your site with their reader base, further accelerating your growth.
- *Adds credibility:* Publishing interviews with recognized experts adds to your site's credibility and trustworthiness. And when

experts create content for your site, its stature will only improve. It's no longer just you or your people helping your base; you've tapped into something bigger.

♦ *Attracts other experts:* When other experts see their peers on your site, they'll be more open to participating. Often, when experts see their respected peers are already there, they will approach you unsolicited and seek to contribute.

♦ *Helps your business stand apart:* The more you work with outside experts, the more you'll stand out as a trusted and deep source of information. This will help differentiate you from your competitors.

A quick word of caution is in order here: Recognize that many experts are overwhelmed with e-mails asking for their help. When you're able to land a busy one, don't abuse the relationship. Don't assume that because an expert agreed to do an interview or craft an article that he or she will be yours forever. An ongoing commitment may be a fully unrealistic expectation.

But you should ask these experts if they found value in the experience. If they did, you might suggest something more for them. Always be thinking about ways you can provide value to your experts.

WHAT YOU CAN DO FOR EXPERTS

Outside experts are people, too. They have their own interests, desires, and challenges. When you work with experts, it's important that *they find value in the exchange.*

This means you'll need to think about why an expert would want to work with you in the first place. Step into their shoes. Try to identify their needs. Is there something you can do to boost their rocket ships?

This process often starts with a little research. For example, if you know an expert has just released a new book, he or she needs exposure for the book.

Bryan Elliott, founder of the regional networking group Linked Orange County, always had his eye on marketing guru Seth Godin. Bryan's goal was to have Seth to speak at one of his events. But Seth always politely turned Bryan down.

But when Bryan discovered Seth would be speaking at the TED Conference in nearby Long Beach—and that he had just released his book *Linchpin: Are You Indispensable?* (Portfolio Hardcover, 2010)—Bryan persuaded Seth to come speak about the book.

Seth received a warm welcome from a huge room full of fans, who all had received copies of his new book. He also gained a lot of exposure to people—many of whom went on to write positive reviews of his book.

Seth subsequently agreed to participate in one of Bryan's future events.

What clinched the deal for Bryan was Seth's desire to promote his book, in concert with the convenience of the experience. The important point here is to make sure you understand the needs and desires of the expert.

Here are some things you can do to help experts:

- *Expose them to your crowd:* If your reader base is composed of people the expert is seeking to reach, explain how working with you will benefit him or her. Explain the makeup of your base and its size. If your base is small, mention some of the expert's peers who have participated in the past.
- *Help promote their latest projects:* If the expert has just launched something new, make it clear that you'd like to talk about that in an interview. For example, Ford's Scott Monty had just launched a new car prior to my interview with him, so I made sure we spoke about the car *and* how the company was promoting it with social media.
- *Recognize their hard work:* Many people desire recognition for their efforts. If an expert has accomplished something significant, consider making that the purpose of a possible interview. Ask questions about how it was done, the lessons learned, the mistakes made, and so on.
- *Make it easy:* Often, experts are highly sought after. They need to be picky about what they choose to do with their limited time. If you can make your request easy for them to fulfill, the chances of them saying yes will increase significantly. For example, I have attended trade events where experts were presenting. I asked for 10-minute interviews on the very topics they were speaking on. Most of the time experts are happy to participate if it just takes a few minutes.

If you want to land experts, you need to focus fully on their needs. Try to identify a few experts you might want to approach. Why would they want to work with you? Look at the preceding list for some ideas.

How to Find and Qualify an Expert

What makes someone an expert? Is there an easy way to determine if an expert is a good fit for your reader base?

Start by reading the expert's written work. Often they will have books, but not always. Many experts are publishing articles on popular sites or their own blogs.

Carefully analyze the substance of what the expert is writing about. Is it new? Has he or she come up with interesting perspectives on common problems your reader base is facing?

If you can't find good experts, you might want to *look at successful businesses*. For example, Starbucks has a really amazing social media program in place. I found Alexandra Wheeler, the digital strategist for Starbucks, presenting at a local event. Although Alexandra was an expert, it was her brand that was known to my audience.

Thus, consider also looking to businesses that are excelling in your space. Then dig to find the people behind the success. Those people make great experts because they rarely get to step out from behind the brand.

Here are a few qualifying questions to ask yourself when seeking experts:

- What knowledge does this person have that my base is seeking?
- Can he or she articulate ideas and concepts that are under-standable?
- Does my reader base know this person?
- Does this person work for a company that is known to my base?
- Does this person have a unique idea he or she can share?
- Do I have any peers I should consider?

There are a number of great resources for finding experts. In Chapter 3, I mentioned a few good ways to find experts, including the Amazon upcoming bestsellers list and conferences. (Turn back to the section on discovering people for more on these sources.)

Another excellent source of experts is Peter Shankman's Help-A-Reporter-Out (HARO) site (see HelpAReporter.com). You may not think of yourself as a reporter. But if you're working on an article and need some expert opinions, HARO is a great place to go. The service is free, and you'll find that a lot of experts will contact you rather quickly.

HOW TO USE OUTSIDE EXPERTS FOR CONTENT

Now that you're convinced of the value of working with outside experts, let's talk about ways to work with them. Experts should always be rooted into your content strategy.

As the elevation principle explains, great content plus other people are the first two areas your business should focus on. Content *by* experts, or focused *on* experts, should become a significant portion of what you produce.

Here are some ways you can work with experts to generate content:

Video interviews: Many experts love seeing themselves on camera. Try to secure video interviews with experts traveling to your neighborhood, or while you're attending a conference. For example, when I learned that Joe Pulizzi (co-author, with Newt Barrett, of *Get Content. Get Customers.*; Voyager Media, Inc., 2008) was speaking at an event in my hometown, I made sure we met up in an empty conference room for a video interview.

Written interviews: Interviews with experts also make for interesting reading. If you can get an expert on the phone, try to record the interview and have it transcribed. For example, I interviewed Andy Sernovitz (author of *Word of Mouth Marketing*) by phone. I asked him to call into a bridge line then recorded the conversation. Once the transcript was complete, I edited it down into a concise article; I also offered the audio recording as an option for people in my reader base who wanted to hear the entire conversation.

Book reviews: A review of an expert's books can become a powerful source of content. Rather than simply read the book and write about it, use it as an excuse to interact with the author. The ideal situation is to get on the phone with the expert. However, e-mail questions can also work. When Guy Kawasaki released his book *Enchantment: The Art of Changing Hearts, Minds, and Actions* (Portfolio Hardcover, 2011), I interviewed him by phone. I asked how he promoted the book, about the concepts of the book, and a few questions related to his thoughts on the future.

Judges for contests: If you decide to run a contest, consider recruiting some experts to become judges. Typically, this is a small commitment for the expert who will gain exposure as a judge. For example, I recruited Ann Handley from MarketingProfs (and co-author, with C.C. Chapman, of *Content Rules*; Wiley, 2010) to be a judge for one of our top 10 blog contests. This added credibility to the contest and brought her valuable exposure to my base.

Expert-penned articles: The ultimate achievement is to have top experts create original content for your site. Sometimes you'll need to start with one of the preceding ideas before you ask them for an article. The easiest experts to land are the ones who need more exposure for their business. Start with a trial article. If the result is well received, consider asking for another. As I mentioned in Chapter 2, I recruited Jay Baer (co-author of *The Now Revolution*) to write for our site very early. His articles were so well received that he began penning a monthly column.

This list is a small sampling of how you could weave outside experts into your content development strategy. Experts bring incalculable credibility to your content efforts.

Be sure to come up with an expert-focused content strategy. When experts are part of your content strategy, you'll have excellent fuel to propel your rocket ship.

Some experts become so instrumental to your business that they fall into a classification of their own: the *fire starters*.

Leveraging Fire Starters

Fire starters are the superheros of your industry. Fire starters are those people who have so much influence that their endorsement can ignite an explosive effect that shoots your rocket ship to new heights nearly overnight.

These experts have direct access to a superengaged reader base that directly matches the base you're seeking to acquire. When fire starters recommend something or someone to their base, it's like dropping a match into kerosene—it ignites with a fury. The result is often immediate: many people become fans of your business because of the power of a fire starter.

If your launch is just getting under way, you'll want to use fire starters to ensure a successful takeoff.

THE INFLUENTIAL POWER OF FIRE STARTERS

Here's a quick story to demonstrate how fire starters can propel your business.

Back in early 2009—before I started SocialMediaExaminer.com—I had the idea of publishing a paper called the *Social Media Marketing Industry Report*. It would be a survey-based report revealing how marketers were using social media.

But I had a big problem: I didn't have access to social media marketers. I only had maybe 500 people following me on Twitter at the time.

I knew I'd need to team up with some superexperts to help get the word out about the report. Specifically, I needed people with influence among social media marketers.

Months earlier, I had targeted three people: Chris Garrett, Denise Wakeman, and Mari Smith. Each had at least 10,000 people following them on Twitter, regularly wrote about the hot social media topics of the day, and had raving fan bases.

I started writing articles about them, positioning them to my reader base as social media experts. I later approached each of them and asked if they'd be willing to help me with my survey.

I explained it would be the beginning of a larger strategy for an upcoming event called the Social Media Success Summit 2009. I invited all three to be key presenters, and offered them a lucrative revenue share of the event. They agreed.

We launched a survey to gather data for the report. In only 10 days 880 social media marketers were participating—mostly powered by my fire starters. Chris, Mari, and Denise also contacted major online publications on my behalf, suggesting an article be written about the final report.

Once the study was complete and the report was released, my fire starters helped promote it. The results were amazing. In a few short weeks more than 40,000 people had read the report, hundreds of publications wrote about it, and for more than a year it appeared on the first page of Google for the search phrase "social media marketing."

Each of these three fire starters also became an instrumental part of the launch of SocialMediaExaminer.com.

TURNING EXPERTS INTO FIRE STARTERS

All fire starters are experts. Not all experts are fire starters. *The best potential fire starters have the eyes and ears of people who closely match your ideal base.* These types of experts have usually been around for a long while and have very large followings.

If you weave working with experts into your marketing strategy, some can be nurtured into fire starters. The key to turning experts into fire starters involves forging a deep and mutually beneficial relationship—and that takes time.

You must bring something to the table that fire starters want. That may include a unique opportunity to be part of something big, or an equity stake in your product, company, or event.

Follow these steps to turn experts into fire starters:

1. *Identify experts who could become fire starters.* As you go about seeking out experts for your content efforts, watch for those who have the makings of a fire starter for your business. Judge the relationship the expert has with his or her reader base. You'll want to focus on those experts who have the greatest influence among people who most closely match your base.

2. *Give the experts what they want—often.* Consider doing multiple interviews and book reviews with this type of expert. Get him or her in front of your audience frequently. The key mantra here is to always *nurture the relationship* with potential fire starters. You want to provide generous value to these types of experts. It becomes a real win-win situation because these experts also resonate with your base.

3. *Attempt a face-to-face connection.* If you have the opportunity to meet the expert in person, take it. Suggest that you grab a

beer, do lunch, or at least visit one of his or her speaking gigs and chat afterward. When experts have an opportunity to connect with you personally, that will deepen the relationship.

4. *Make an offer.* If the relationship between the two of you has grown—and the outcome has become mutually beneficial—consider asking for something. Propose your idea to the expert. Don't expect an immediate yes. And be okay with a no. Remember that you've built a great relationship with an expert that has been mutually beneficial. Today's no could become a yes tomorrow.

5. *Repeat the process.* Target new experts who could become future fire starters for your business.

Keep this process in the back of your mind whenever you seek out experts. Some relationships will blossom into powerful alliances that can quickly accelerate the speed and height of your rocket ship.

Why Focus on Other People?

When you serve others, you'll grow. It really is that simple.

People want meaningful insight, access to great people, and recognition.

Your reader base wants to learn how to solve their problems. They love hearing from other people who can help them. Often, those other people are outside experts.

Experts have problems they want solved, as well. And they love recognition.

You need to know precisely what your reader base wants. You also must know the needs of experts.

When you shift your mind-set and your marketing strategy toward meeting the needs of others, you'll quickly grow a following that will evangelize your business.

Your base has an unprecedented ability to quickly share your outstanding content with their friends and fans. What ensues is a ripple effect that can take your rocket ship higher and higher.

Some experts will become fire starters. When that happens, your reader base will grow even more quickly.

I encourage you to embrace the principle of focusing your content on other people. In future chapters I'll provide plenty of details to help you create this type of content.

■ ■ ■

This chapter examined the power of other people—a key component of the elevation principle. It revealed how to identify your ideal reader base, made the case for using outside experts, and showed you the power of fire starters. The chapter also took a close look at how to find and use outside experts.

You should now have a clear profile of your ideal base, and have identified some outside experts you'd like to work with.

In the next chapter I will show you how to engage other people.

Actively Engaging Other People

You get the best out of others when you give the best of yourself.
—Harvey S. Firestone

When you think of the word "engage," what metaphors come to mind? Perhaps a spark plug igniting the fuel that starts an engine? The intense focus of two people in deep discussion? Or the excitement a couple feels as they move one step closer to marriage?

People don't engage as often as they'd like to. But when they do, they experience a deep sense of connection and satisfaction. For your business, engaging your reader base (and other experts) will be what sets it apart. When engaged, people transform from passive observers to active participants—and they'll be happy to help take your rocket ship to new heights.

In the prior chapter I explained the power of other people, and how to find them. Embracing the strength of others is an important component of the elevation principle. But how do you go from identifying others to actively engaging them? What can you do to increase your chances of success with other people?

When people are engaged, they rapidly consume your content, burning your fuel. This quickly propels your rocket ship forward. If they're not engaged, your ship will never leave the ground.

This chapter will reveal ways you can enhance your connections with your base and experts. It will explore human behavior and psychology, as well as debunk a common marketing misconception that can prevent your business from achieving success.

Reciprocity Marketing

Perhaps you're familiar with the rule of reciprocity eloquently described by Robert Cialdini is his book *Influence*.[1] He defines a persuasive rule that transcends borders and culture.

The rule of reciprocity asserts that people are hardwired to respond to a favor or gift by returning one of their own. Cialdini argues that this internal obligation to reciprocate is nearly beyond our control.

Here are two examples of how the rule works, from Cialdini's book.

Two students were taking part in a study focused on art appreciation—or so it seemed. Their task was to rate the quality of some paintings.

In the middle of the study, one of the students (called Joe, by Cialdini) left the room and returned with two cans of Coke. As Joe entered the room, he said, "I asked him [the experimenter] if I could get myself a Coke, and he said it was okay, so I bought one for you, too."

Joe was not an unknowing subject, however. In reality, he was a critical part of the experiment.

Later, Joe asked a favor of the person who received the Coke. Joe explained he needed to sell raffle tickets, and asked the subject to help him by purchasing some tickets.

The true purpose of the experiment was to measure whether an unspoken obligation existed between the giver (Joe) and the receiver. The research was repeated over and over again with different subjects.

---

[1] Cialdini, R.B. *Influence: Science and Practice.* (New York: HarperCollins, 3rd ed., 1993).

The results were undeniable: *Those people who received a free Coke purchased twice as many raffle tickets as those who never received a Coke.*

Cialdini also claimed that the reciprocity rule doesn't apply only to one-on-one relationships.

In 1985, Ethiopia was one of the poorest nations in the world. With a dwindling food supply and an economy in ruin, the country was in dire need. Its population was rapidly dying of disease and starvation.

That same year, Mexico City experienced a major earthquake. Ethiopian officials decided to send $5,000 in relief donations to the country of Mexico, to aid in its recovery.

Cialdini was perplexed as to why such a poor and needy country would send money to another, richer, country. He decided to investigate the matter further and discovered something fascinating: Fifty years earlier, Mexico had assisted Ethiopia when it was invaded by Italy.

Cialdini postulated that *despite the enormous needs of Ethiopians, they also needed to reciprocate a gift they had received decades earlier.*

These two examples demonstrate the power of the rule of reciprocity.

In the first example, the subject was unknowingly manipulated, with the goal of forcing a response: to purchase raffle tickets. In the second example, however, Ethiopians did something that appeared irrational, given their circumstances. They gave money to pay back a very old favor they had received.

Can the rule of reciprocity help your business? Should it be employed? Are there dangers?

WHAT'S WRONG WITH RECIPROCATION MARKETING?

If the rule of reciprocity is true—and I have no doubt it is—should businesses use it to their gain? Should you start employing reciprocity experiments with your reader base?

There's no question that, in the second example, Ethiopia had received a gift many decades earlier from Mexico. It also appeared that the subjects in Joe's experiments, in the first example, were receiving gifts. The difference is that in the case of Joe, the subjects were manipulated to act. In contrast, following Mexico's original gift, there was never an expectation that Ethiopia would reciprocate.

Cialdini acknowledges that salespeople could easily exploit the rule of reciprocity. Indeed, this rule has been aggressively applied to modern sales and marketing efforts.

In many ways, reciprocity has become a curse. Businesses often use gift-giving as a way to obligate people to respond—to force an unnatural response.

Each time you walk into a car dealership, watch for the extended hand of a salesperson offering a free can of soda. If you work for a big corporation, those exclusive game tickets from a vendor are another example. What used to be gifts have been transformed into manipulative acts of persuasion.

The rule of reciprocity has even corrupted America's pharmaceutical industry. In 2008, the industry self-imposed gift-giving restrictions to prevent doctors from feeling obligated to prescribe medications manufactured by companies bearing gifts.

Here's where businesses get it wrong: Knowing about the rule of reciprocity is one thing; expecting something in return for your efforts is an entirely different matter.

I believe that Mexico gave a *genuine gift* to Ethiopia, never expecting to receive anything in return. But something did return when Mexico was in need. The issue here comes down to *motive* and *intention*.

When a gift is actually a marketing message in disguise, don't be surprised when people don't engage or reciprocate.

Overemploying these tactics will repel your reader base. When they stop consuming your content, your rocket ship will lose its forward momentum—and could come crashing down.

Today (largely due to the work of experts like Cialdini) both consumers and marketers are more familiar with the rule of reciprocity. Marketers try to tap the rule's power. Consumers are wiser to the tricks of marketers—and can defend against them.

Given the widespread distrust of businesses, is it really wise to engage in an activity that could be perceived as manipulative by your reader base?

"In sales circles, reciprocity is often employed as the *Give and Take, Take, Take* strategy, due to our propensity to continue complying with requests even after only one initial favor from the salesperson. Truly successful businesses know better. To rephrase marketing guru

Jay Abraham's strategy of preeminence, you should give, give, give, and your profits will explode," explained Brian Clark.[2]

It's okay to give away freebies, but make sure you can distinguish gifts from marketing messages.

At SocialMediaExaminer.com, we give away a free social media tutorial to people who sign up for our e-mail newsletter. I have no illusions about the fact that some people sign up to get the tutorial and then immediately unsubscribe.

Our free tutorial is *not a gift*. Why not? People are purchasing it with their name and e-mail address. Thus, they have fulfilled their obligation by simply filling out the form. It's a *transparent exchange*, but not a gift.

Should your business give gifts to your base? Is there something beneficial you can take from the rule of reciprocity—without violating your conscience?

The Importance of Giving Genuine Gifts

There's no question that people love receiving gifts. If you want to capture the attention of people and fully engage them, then give them great gifts.

The question is, what is a real gift? And how do you give one to your reader base and experts?

True gifts engage people and help build relationships.

A gift is something given without expectation of anything in return. The recipient does not earn it. Gifts show your appreciation, or provide no-strings-attached gestures of assistance.

If you give a gift hoping the receiver will give one back, that's not a gift, it's an exchange. *Gifts are not transactions*. Gifts are free of obligation or expectations of reciprocity.

Genuine gifts can't be wrapped in marketing messages. Rather, they are wrapped transparently, without obvious motives or pitches.

Gifts don't need to be costly. Indeed, sometimes the smallest gestures can go a long way. Modern technology has made it very easy for businesses to give great gifts.

---

[2] Clark, B. "Much Obliged: The Power of Reciprocity," www.copyblogger.com/much-obliged-the-power-of-reciprocity/*Copyblogger,* February 2006.

"The Internet (and digital goods) has lowered the marginal cost of generosity," said Seth Godin. "Giving a gift makes you indispensable. Inventing a gift, creating art—that is what the market seeks out, and the givers are the ones who earn our respect and attention."[3]

When your ideal base is receiving genuine gifts from you, they'll find great value in the relationship, helping your rocket ship make forward progress.

THE THREE GIFT CIRCLES

Seth Godin describes three concentric circles of people we give gifts to. Understanding these circles will help you rethink your gift-giving efforts.

The first, smaller inner circle contains our *family, friends, and coworkers*. These are the people we typically think of giving gifts to during birthdays and holidays. For example, if friends come over for dinner, you wouldn't charge them for the meal; it's your gift to them.

And gifts focused on the inner circle can be very small acts.

"One of the greatest gifts I received was when a friend did my dishes (huge pile, in the sink . . .). It seems ridiculously simple but it was something I needed, something I never expected, and most importantly something that told me—without words—that he was thinking of me and wanted to help me. It made me feel special," said Amy Parmenter.[4]

The second circle is the *circle of commerce*. In this circle are the people and organizations that pay us for our work. They're the people you might send boxes of chocolates to as a way of saying thanks for being great customers.

We too often focus on this commerce circle. We give to this circle with the hope to get more from them later. Godin explains that when our mission is solely focused on this circle, our giving suffers and, ultimately, so does the business.

Godin refers to the third and outer circle as *"friendlies."* These people include your reader base and other experts. Today, friendlies make up a much larger group, due to social media. The power of giving to this circle is significant, yet it's a gifting circle that most businesses ignore.

---

[3] Godin, S. *Linchpin: Are You Indispensable?* (New York: Penguin Group, 2010).

[4] Stelzner, M. "What Is the Greatest Gift You Have Ever Received?," Social Media Examiner, December 25, 2010.

Here are a few examples of the power of giving gifts to your base: Alexander Kenter explains:

When I first started out as a freelance copywriter, I received truck-loads of advertisements and mailings from companies that were all eager to make me their client. I got letters from Web designers, administration agencies, banks, lawyers, insurers, printers, computer resellers, and what-have-you. And I got a pen. I received a pen from a company that sold customizable, promotional giveaway pens. And this one already had the name of my freelance company on it. That was the moment that for me it all became real. It was highly ingratiating to see something so simple, yet so personal.[5]

Here's another example:

In 1978, Ben & Jerry's opened an ice cream store in an abandoned gas station in Burlington, Virginia. During the summer, they projected free movies on the outside wall of the gas station.

"Crowds showed up for every movie, with blankets and beach chairs," explained Albert Grande, a local resident at the time. "Ben & Jerry's turned their parking lot into a miniature drive-in theater. The crowds ordered a lot of ice cream. They all told many of their friends about Ben and Jerry's."[6]

Google is another excellent example. It has grown into a power-house by giving away amazing applications that go way beyond its search engine. Maps, word processors, calendars, books, e-mail, video (think YouTube), news, and translation software—just to mention a few—are provided at absolutely no cost to Google's base.

To summarize, here are the three circles of gifts:

- ◆ *First circle:* Your friends, family, and colleagues. These are people you have an intimate connection with.
- ◆ *Second circle:* Your paying customers and business partners. These are people who have a direct impact on your revenue.
- ◆ *Third circle:* Your base and outside experts. This is a very large group of people, many you'll never know personally.

---

[5] Ibid.

[6] Grande, A. *When You Give, You Get: The Law of Reciprocity* (grandepublishing.com, 2007).

Godin argues you should focus on the first and third circles, not the second. Your generosity in these circles will lead to deeper engagement and more income.

"As the third circle grows in size, the second circle takes care of itself . . . because as you give more and more to friendlies, the list of people you do your work for always grows," explained Godin.[7]

Giving real gifts to your base and experts should be a key part of your business strategy. When you give gifts without motives, people notice. When the gifts are valuable to your reader base, they'll let their friends know. You'll build your base and your business.

Here's an example of the type of impact gift-giving can have on your reader base. This is an actual e-mail received from someone in my base (whose name I have omitted for privacy reasons):

> *I feel that I owe you something for everything I have learned from you. I guess what I am trying to say is, if you ever need me to do something for you in Vancouver just let me know. I am open to anything you might have in mind. For instance, if there is anyone in the Vancouver area that you might want to give a free ticket to your summit coming up, I would personally go and deliver it to them, completely gift-wrapped with a Starbucks coffee; or if it's a woman, with some flowers. You pick the request, and I will devote a full day to anything that you want.*
>
> *A loyal follower in Vancouver!!!*

It should be clear to you that giving gifts to the right people develops a loyal fan base. That base will be what helps your rocket ship achieve speeds and heights you could never imagine.

What gifts should you give to your base?

How to Give Gifts

As I noted at the beginning of the chapter, the gifts you give to others don't need to be expensive or complicated. The Internet has made it very easy to give low-cost yet highly valuable gifts.

The content you create is your gift to your reader base. Two simple examples include creating a valuable video or writing a detailed blog

---

[7] Godin, S. *Linchpin.*

post. In either case, you could show your base how to solve a common problem they face. When there's no marketing messages wrapped around this type of content, it is a gift.

As you share gifts with your base, they'll let others know about you.

When you provide outstanding content for free, you're giving a gift to your ideal base. Why? *Often, great content is not readily available for free and without any strings attached.* Instead, people typically must purchase such knowledge from experts or other sources.

When you give away great content, you provide your base something they desire, drawing them closer to you. And some people will reciprocate by referring your content to a friend or purchasing your products. But even if they don't reciprocate, chances are they'll keep coming back.

The key is to *give without expectation of reciprocation.* Yes, you know there will be a response, but don't expect one. No one is obligated to respond when you give a gift. If they were obligated, it wouldn't be a gift. But if you give the right gifts, people will respond.

This applies to experts, as well. Interviewing an expert and publishing the interview is a gift when there's nothing expected in return. It's a gift to the expert because he or she is getting free exposure to your base. It's a gift to your base because the expert is sharing unique knowledge that most people don't have access to.

Here are a few examples of the many ways to give gifts.

Publicly Recognize the Outstanding Efforts of Others   Recognition can come in many forms, and can involve your base or experts. If someone in your industry has accomplished something notable, consider acknowledging it to your base.

If you have a Facebook fan who is constantly helping answer other people's questions, why not declare that person a fan of the month? Alternatively, consider writing an article showcasing a successful company and sharing the behind-the-scenes story with your base.

At SocialMediaExaminer.com, we regularly watch for businesses that are achieving success with social media. For example, when a hostile gunman took over the Discovery Channel headquarters, we shared a behind-the-scenes story. We showed how social media helped employees keep in contact with friends and family, and how businesses can use these tools in emergency situations.

Help People Solve Their Problems   There are many different ways you can help people. Start by creating content that solves the challenges faced by your base. This could include screen-capture videos showing step-by-step processes or detailed articles.

You can extend this to one-on-one help. Make a point of replying to comments on your blog and offering assistance to people who post questions on social media sites.

When it comes to experts, you can also ask how you can help *them*. Sometimes the simple question, "How can I help you?" (when asked without a motive) can go a long way.

Promote Other People's Content   Every time you share a great link to some relevant content, you're giving two gifts: one to your base and the other to the person or company that created the content.

For example, SocialMediaExaminer.com has more than 50 contributing writers—many of whom have their own blogs. We regularly scour those writer's blogs looking for great content we can share. When we find something useful, we share links back to those blog articles with our base. Our base loves great content and the authors enjoy the added exposure.

Experts also love it when people promote their content. Be sure to share some of it with your base.

The key to sharing other people's content is to *not ask for reciprocation, nor to expect it.*

Every time your reader base finds great value in the content you provide them, their opinion of your business improves. This can have a significant impact on the growth and propulsion of your rocket ship.

Remember, it's people who take your business to new places. When you give them what they want, your business will grow.

Think of the types of gifts you could provide to your base: What does your base value? What can you give? How can you ensure that what you're giving is really a gift? Write down a few ideas.

Using Social Proof

Giving gifts is merely one way to engage your base. Another powerful motivator is the concept of *social proof.*

When you were a kid, did you ever get swindled? "I'll trade you this big penny for that little dime. . . . " When I went to a fair a few years back with my family, I saw something that surprised me.

A group of people were in a frenzy standing by a big wall of computer monitors, where some were taking surveys using touch-screen displays. As part of the surveys, they were inputting their household income, age, phone number, and interest in buying certain types of products.

Why were at least 20 people always in line in front of these machines? Because by completing the digital survey, they received a free pass to come back to the fair over the next 25 days.

My mom was one of the people in line. Afterward I asked her, "Why did you give them all of that personal information?"

She said, "You know, I probably shouldn't have. But I saw everyone else doing it, and I got some tickets. But I'll most likely never use them."

By the way, each ticket was worth $9 and worked only with valid photo identification!

When people are not sure about something, they often look to the behaviors and actions of others. Thus, *social proof is the process of validating an action by looking to the actions taken by others.* Some people have referred to this concept as the "herd mentality."

The premise is that people make snap judgments regarding whether they should stop and do something different, based on what others are doing.

When people see lots of others supporting your content, many will quickly do the same, accelerating your propulsion.

Here are some examples.

Scientist Stanley Milgram and his team decided to see if they could get busy New York City passersby to aimlessly stare at the sky. First they had one man look into the air for a full minute. Everyone simply passed him right by.

But when the scientific team placed five people gazing into the empty sky, the number of passersby who stopped and stared with them more than quadrupled.[8]

For a business example, consider McDonald's. Have you ever seen the large yellow letters, "Over 99 Billion Served"? McDonald's has been displaying numbers on its signs since the 1960s.

Now you might be wondering, "What does any of this mean to my business?"

Science has shown that most people are followers. They look to the wisdom of crowds or other similar people to help them make decisions. "Since 95 percent of the people are imitators and only 5 percent initiators, people are persuaded more by the actions of others than by any proof we can offer," explained sales expert Cavett Robert.[9]

In the case of the sky gawkers, busy New Yorkers stopped and stared because they saw others like them doing the same thing. The mental trigger in their minds might have gone something like this: "Hmm. Everyone seems to be looking into the sky. I wonder what they are looking at? I'll look, too."

For McDonald's it's a similar story. When a hungry family is driving down the street, they're offered many options. Just under the golden arches are those big numbers showing how many people have been served. That is a *proof mechanism*. The thought process of the driver might go like this: "If that many people have eaten there, I guess I can't go wrong."

Employing social proof mechanisms can turn people from disengaged passersby into active participants.

In the case of your business, it could encourage people to make decisions as simple as sharing your content on Facebook, leaving a comment, or deciding to subscribe to your e-mail updates. Any of these behaviors would add further social proof for other people and encourage more of them to engage.

---

[8] Goldstein, N.J., Martin, S.J., & Cialdini, R.B. *Yes! 50 Scientifically Proven Ways to Be Persuasive.* (New York: Free Press, 2008).

[9] Cialdini, R.B. *Influence.*

"From a marketing standpoint, social proof is the basis of both buzz and large sales figures. Without it, there'd be no 'grapevine' in the first place," explained Brian Clark.[10]

And the more you employ social proof, the more people will activate with your content.

Here are two more examples:

Amazon's product ranking system: Amazon employs a number of different social proof mechanisms to help consumers make decisions. It allows people to rate and review all of its products. It also shows the sales rankings of products in similar categories. Both of these help consumers speed the decision-making process by showing how popular a product is.

Bestseller book covers: Have you ever seen the tagline "More than 1 million copies sold!" on the cover of a book? When you're looking for something new to read, you might be more inclined to select the book that so many others have purchased.

Social proof helps grow the size of your rocket ship. When people see tons of others onboard, they'll be more likely to subscribe or regularly read your content.

How can you employ social proof to help your business grow?

How to Employ Social Proof on Your Site

From a marketing perspective, social proof involves displaying numbers and the right words. Those words are carefully crafted copy designed to stimulate action or affinity; or they could be in the form of testimonials.

The best way to demonstrate social proof is to look at it in action. Here's how SocialMediaExaminer.com uses social proof—and how you can, too.

Numbers of Subscribers We boldly plaster the words "Join 59,000+ of your peers! Get our latest articles delivered to your e-mail

---

[10] Clark, B. "Social Proof: Herd It through the Grapevine," *Copyblogger,* February 28, 2006. www.copyblogger.com/social-proof-herd-it-through-the-grapevine/.

inbox . . . " on a subscription box on each and every page of our Web site. The number shows that a lot of people subscribe, and the words "your peers" imply that people just like you subscribe.

You could do the same on your subscriber forms. Some e-mail service providers have little counters that display the growing number automatically. Alternatively, you can simply create some text that shows the most up-to-date number.

Tweet Numbers We clearly display the number of retweets our articles have received at the top of each article. On any given day that number ranges from 300 to 1,000. As people visit the site they see that number as proof that the article must be valuable. It often triggers more retweets and longer times spent reading the article.

Twitter provides a simple plugin that will automatically count and display the number of tweets linking to any given page. It is very easy to add to your site. Simply search for "retweet button" to add it.

Facebook Share Numbers In multiple locations on our site we display the number of people who have shared or liked our content on Facebook. The Facebook plugin also reveals the names of people you know who have also shared the content.

Facebook does all the heavy lifting, counting the number of actions and dynamically displaying names of people in your network who acted. Search for the "Facebook like button" to add it.

Facebook Fans On every page we display a box that shows how many people are fans of our Facebook page, along with the faces of a few (see Figure 5.1). This is a powerful double-dose of social proof because Facebook shows the faces and names of people in your personal network who are also fans of the page. When new visitors see friends or people just like them, they'll likely become more engaged.

This is very easy to add to any site. You'll grow your Facebook fan base and provide powerful social proof to people who visit your site. You can add this to your site by searching for "Facebook like box."

FIGURE 5.1   Notice the arrows pointing to social proof embedded on
SocialMediaExaminer.com.

E-mail Social Proof   At the very top of every one of our daily e-mail
blasts we post text that reads: "Serving 59,000+ subscribers daily."
This serves a few purposes. It reinforces that people who have
subscribed made the right decision. It also discourages people from
unsubscribing because so many of their peers are already there.

   If you have a decent number of subscribers, you should consider
adding similar language to the opening of your e-mails.

Awards   On our "About Us" page we include mentions of relevant
awards and achievements. For example, we state that Technorati and
Advertising Age rank us as one of the top 25 business blogs in the
world. We also have a video that shows me talking about this
achievement while driving my car. During the video, relevant screenshots display the awards.

   Many times organizations that rank or award top Web sites provide
a small badge of honor you can place on your site. Those awards serve

as another form of social proof because they show that others have recognized your content. If you have achieved any rankings or awards, consider displaying them on your site.

Testimonials As part of the celebration of SocialMediaExaminer .com's one-year anniversary, a number of known experts in our industry recorded happy birthday video messages. We combined them into a video montage and displayed it on our site. Experts congratulating us on our success serve as powerful social proof.

You should consider soliciting experts for endorsements. You don't need to make a video. You can simply ask for a few sentences via e-mail. When you get them, add them to your site.

■ ■ ■

The preceding examples are a small sampling of the many ways you can employ social proof triggers to encourage your base to act.

Can social proof also help you when working with experts?

How to Use Social Proof to Persuade Experts

Social proof cues are a powerful way to engage and retain your reader base. But the power of social proof doesn't stop with your base. It can also help you persuade experts.

Experts use social proof to make decisions in the same ways that your base does. When you reach out to an expert, you'll want to convey that their peers are working with you, or that you have a large base that would be interested in hearing from the expert.

For example, when I reached out to Seth Godin for an interview, I provided a link to Technorati showing we had the number-one small business blog in the world, at that moment. This made his decision very easy, because small business owners were one of his targets for his new book, *Linchpin*.

Alternatively, when I reached out Chris Brogan for an interview, I provided him with a link to the interview I did with Seth Godin and some of his other peers.

The take-home message here is to leverage names, numbers, and awards to engage experts.

Experts are often very short on time and make snap judgments based on the *perceived value of the opportunity.* Never assume they know you or have heard of your site. By providing social proof information, experts are more likely to say yes. Their mental process is often something like this: "I respect that other expert. Maybe I should participate, too." The assumption is that you have been vetted by their peers and thus should be considered.

Here are a few ways you can use social proof to persuade an expert:

Mention the size of your base: Numbers are very persuasive. Be sure to specify critical numbers, such as number of subscribers or monthly page views. For example, "Our nearly 60,000 e-mail subscribers would love to hear from you." If you can, elaborate to make the statistic more relevant to the expert. For example, "Our site has 500,000 monthly page views, composed mostly of marketers and small business owners."

Drop names of the expert's peers: Names also bring a lot of power. If you have recently interviewed a known expert or company representative, be sure to mention that person in your communications. For example, "We've interviewed your peers from Starbucks, H&R Block, Ford, and the U.S. Navy."

Mention relevant awards: If your business or site has won any awards that might be known to the expert, be sure to call attention to them. For example, "Our site is one of the top 25 business blogs in the world, according to Technorati."

You might feel a little awkward tooting your own horn, but chances are, you've got only one shot to convince an expert. Bring out the big guns of social proof to help close the deal.

Employing social proof with your base and experts is a powerful way to engage them, helping you grow your business quickly.

What types of social proof can you use for your business? What numbers can you share? Have you worked with big names or big businesses? Have you received any awards? Start adding social proof to your site and watch what happens.

Social proof helps attract readers and experts to your rocket ship. Employ these techniques to help your business soar.

Giving gifts and employing social proof are compelling strategies to draw people to your business. But is there anything else you can do to get people engaged with your business?

Moving People to Action

Moving people from passive lurkers to active participants is often a difficult process.

Think about it: What's your favorite movie or book? Have you ever contacted the film producer or the book author and let him or her know how much you enjoyed his or her work? What about your favorite Web site? How often do you leave a comment on a company's page?

If you're like most people, you never bother to act on something you enjoy or find valuable—even when you want to or know you should.

There's some interesting psychological research that explains why we fail to do this. The research also demonstrates a persuasive approach for convincing people to act.

In 1963, a research team led by Howard Leventhal proved that the last thing you put in writing has a big impact.[11] The story involves tetanus shots and Yale University students.

The students were given booklets describing and showing the consequences of tetanus disease. The goal was to convince subjects to get a free tetanus shot at the campus clinic.

Only 3 percent acted and got the shot.

Leventhal's team decided to run a parallel study, in this case simply adding the following to the end of the materials:

- ◆ A map of the school with a circle around the health care facility
- ◆ A written description of the location
- ◆ The hours when the free shots were administered

The result: a 900 percent improvement! A remarkable 28 percent of students got the tetanus shots, up from only 3 percent.

---

[11] Leventhal, H., Singer, R., & Jones, S. "Effects of Fear and Specificity of Recommendation upon Attitudes and Behavior," *Journal of Personality and Social Psychology,* July 1965. http://www.rutgers.academia.edu/HowardLeventhal/Papers/203045/Effects_of_Fear_and_Specificity_of_Recommendation_Upon_Attitudes_and_Behavior.

Why did so many more students act in the parallel experiment? The clear and straightforward guidance made it effortless for them to get their tetanus shots. They could easily act.

This study is a dramatic example of why providing a very clear next step to people will significantly increase their likelihood of taking action.

If *you want people to act, tell them what to do.* This guidance is known in marketing circles as the *call to action.*

Lesson from Two Hawaiian Girls

I remember landing in Maui a few years ago. While working our way to the rental car area, I was struck by something—almost literally. Two attractive Hawaiian girls were standing there.

One girl said, "Coupons to restaurants," as she handed me a little booklet. The other said, "Maps of Maui," her hand outstretched.

I immediately tossed the coupons in a nearby trash can and kept the handout with the maps. This turned out to be a magazine almost entirely full of advertisements and only a few maps.

Nevertheless, I had an immediate need, and the maps were handed to me at the perfect location. As I went to pick up the rental car, the company also offered different advertorials with maps. However, I turned them away as I already had one I was happy with.

That map magazine stayed in my car the entire time I was in Maui.

At one point, one of my kids fell asleep in the car, and what did I do? I read that magazine from cover to cover—the very thing the advertisers hoped I would do.

CALL TO ACTION DEFINED

The call to action is a specific instruction to your base. It's nothing more than a sign that says, essentially, "Stop what you're doing right now and do this instead." *A call to action is a suggested activity that guides people toward an outcome.*

You're probably very familiar with calls to action in traditional advertising. Think of those commercials that say, "Come in for a free test drive," or "The first 10 callers receive a free paring knife." These types of action requests are very popular in passive media like television, radio, and print advertising.

For online marketing, calls to action can be something as simple as a button that reads "Sign Up for Free," "Join Today," or "Donate Now."

As the Leventhal study demonstrated, if you skip this step, you're leaving people with no clear direction. The result: They will move on.

In the context of your rocket ship, this can lead to complete abandonment. Although you might have outstanding content, without providing your ideal base a tangible reason to return, they likely never will.

Include calls to action in all the content you create. Without a call to action, you're throwing away opportunity. Think of all the people enjoying your content. Because you didn't give them any clear reason to take a next step, they might just say, "That was interesting. I'm going to move on with my day." They may have the best of intentions but never act.

In contrast, if you give people a very clear next step, they might stop what they're doing in their busy day and actually take that step.

For your business, it's essential to employ calls to action among all of your critical content. The types of actions you'll ask for depend on your goals.

Here are some common activities that deserve calls to action:

◆ Register for our free newsletter.
◆ Click here for access to special content.
◆ Join us on Facebook.
◆ Call this number to speak with a sales representative.
◆ Use this coupon code for a special discount.
◆ Schedule an appointment.
◆ Purchase now by clicking here.
◆ Visit our Web site for more information.

Notice how each of these statements begins with an action command. Here's the key: Calls to actions must be very simple, and they must be engaging.

At SocialMediaExaminer.com we use calls to action primarily to grow our e-mail subscriber base. We employ a number of calls to action at key strategic locations (and times) within our content. Model your calls to action based on these examples:

Popup subscription box: For first-time visitors to the site, we use a box that pops up after a short period of time. It says, "Get original Social Media Examiner content sent straight to your e-mail inbox for free." We also offer a free video tutorial as further incentive for people to opt in. A significant 74 percent of all of our subscribers have double opted in to our newsletter using this popup box.

Integrated subscription box: On every single page of our Web site we have a box that encourages people to sign up for our newsletter. It has similar language to the popup box. The words "Subscribe now" are enclosed in a bright orange button. This form is designed as a constant reminder to people that we offer a free e-mail subscription option.

Top navigation: We embed the words "Free Subscription" into our top navigation bar on each page of our site. It is the very first option after the home button. It is placed in such a prominent position because our objective is to grow our base.

Updates banner: We have designed a graphical header near the top of the screen that includes an icon of an envelope and a few social media channels where folks can subscribe for updates.

Whether or not your goal is to grow a subscriber base, you can use these examples to spur ideas for your site.

Calls to action can also be used to encourage other types of activity on your site. Here are a few examples:

Encouraging comments: For bloggers, comments are almost a form of currency. Some blogs seem to have a lot more comments than others. If you want people to comment, the best thing to do is send out a strong call to action at the end of your articles. For example, "What are your thoughts? Do you agree or disagree? Please leave your comment in the box below."

Start with a few questions that encourage a response by your base. Then tell them precisely what to do. I know it sounds crazy, but we've tested this to remarkable success. When we ask people to leave a comment in the box below, the number who do greatly increases.

Growing a Facebook following: Your business may want to use a social media network like Facebook to grow a community. In addition to the Facebook Like box mentioned earlier, you can also create a graphic that simply says, "Join us on Facebook." This straightforward call to action hinges on the word "join," not a more passive verb like "follow."

Viewing special content: If you have developed content that serves as your nuclear fuel, you should consider creating a graphical banner that points people to it. That banner can live on all pages of your site, but should contain a strong call to action. For example, on SocialMediaExaminer.com, we have posted a banner that reads: "Download Social Media Marketing Industry Report."

A clear call to action, placed in strategic locations, will substantially increase the likelihood that people will act. Remember that the action needs to be appealing and effortless.

The more people act, the more others will act. This compounding effect will lead to more upward movement of your rocket ship.

What calls to action can you embed on your site? Write down a few ideas. Now begin implementing them as your call to action.

Why Engage?

If you want to sustain long-term business growth, you'll need to figure out a way to connect with people.

The days of broadcasting one-way marketing messages to consumers are ending. Manipulative reciprocation attempts often result in general distrust and your base questioning your motives.

Instead, by giving genuine gifts to your base and experts—without expecting anything in return—you'll draw people to you in droves. Many will be happy to help share your great content, and some will become loyal customers for life.

Adding social proof mechanisms to your Web site will help turn lurkers into subscribers, commenters, and sharers of your content. It will also help justify people's decision to participate. This can produce a cyclical pattern that draws even more people to your business, propelling your rocket ship.

Finally, by employing strong and relevant calls to action, you'll greatly increase the number of people who act. This means more comments, more subscribers, more fans, and more experts agreeing to work with you.

I encourage you to study these psychological principles in action. Watch for them next time you visit a successful Web site. Then begin applying them to your business.

■ ■ ■

This chapter demonstrated the power of giving gifts, using social proof, and employing strong calls to action. It also revealed the improper use of the rule of reciprocity. By employing these principles, you can achieve a dramatic rise in the engagement and activities of your base.

You should now have some clear ideas that you can begin implementing on your own site.

In Chapter 6 I will demonstrate why content should be at the center of your marketing efforts.

Making Content the Fuel of Your Marketing

Only those who will risk going too far can possibly find out how far one can go.

—T. S. Eliot

Content is the ultimate fuel for launching your rocket ship into space. Why? Outstanding content attracts people in ways that ads, billboards, or commercials never could.

Great content is food for the mind. It feeds the deep desires of people. It enriches lives, solves problems, educates, and even entertains. Great content has a magnetic quality that points the internal compasses of people directly toward your business.

In this chapter I will show you some examples of great content that focuses on other people and lacks any obvious marketing messages. I'll also examine what makes content great and discuss how to craft your content plan.

Proof That Content Works

What follows are two excellent examples of businesses using compelling content. The first one is from a multibillion dollar corporation and the second from a mom living on the range. In both cases, you'll see how these successful businesses have used content focused on other people as the center point of their marketing, while using minimal marketing messages.

Be sure to carefully examine each of these examples, while thinking of ways your business could adopt a similar model.

Man of the House

Procter & Gamble (P&G) makes a wide range of consumer products, some of which appeal to men—and more specifically, dads. Part of P&G's marketing involves finding and working with bloggers. However, its marketers recognized that very few blogs were directed solely at dads.

In 2010, P&G observed that, due to a bad economy, a lot more men were out of work and were seen more often frequenting shopping aisles. The company needed a way to connect with these men. So in June of 2010, it partnered with Barefoot Proximity to produce an online magazine called Man of the House (see ManOfTheHouse.com).

"We saw this need among guys, in particular dads, whose lives had changed, and their role in the family was very different than [the one] their dads typically played," explained Jeannie Tharrington, a P&G spokeswoman.[1]

Now, you might be thinking that a big company like P&G would craft content designed to sell its products, like Gillette razors, Head & Shoulders shampoo, Bounty paper towels, Tide detergent, or Charmin toilet paper. Instead, it created something that had only subtle traces of P&G's involvement. The only reference is a copyright notice in the footer mentioning Barefoot Proximity and P&G Productions.

For Man of the House, the company selected topics men care about, such as food, money, technology, parenting, and relationships (see Figure 6.1).

When you visit the site, the P&G brand is listed nowhere. There's only a single ad for products guys might be interested in, like

---

[1] Neff, J. "Oh Man, Life May Be Tough But Marketers Still Love You," *Advertising Age,* October 11, 2010. adage.com/article/news/marketing-men-a-prime-target-tougher-lives/146396/.

FIGURE 6.1 P&G's Man of the House site covers topics guys care about, while subtly placing ads for company products off to the side.

Source: Reproduced by permission from The Procter & Gamble Company © June 26, 2010.

Gillette razors. And when the site first launched, it contained no advertisements.

"Consumers are getting savvy and are ignoring push marketing. We needed to take a different approach—one that pulled in the consumer by creating a conversation and making it relevant," said David Germano, general manager of Barefoot Proximity, the agency that spawned the initial idea and manages the site for P&G.

According to Germano, Man of the House draws more than 500,000 people each month—and at the time of my interview with Germano, the site was only six months old.

P&G does not advertise Man of the House, either. All traffic comes from relationships with experts and content marketing. "We've established and leveraged relationships with blogger dads," said Germano.

Articles on Man of the House have no correlation to P&G products. Rather, the content is designed to resonate with the lifestyle issues faced by its audience. The site produces highly relevant and educational content that lacks an obvious sales and marketing message.

"We don't just talk about being dads, we talk about being men. Integrity is huge. We're genuine and helpful," explained Craig Heimbuch, the site's editor-in-chief.

Here's how the purpose of Man of the House is described on the Web site:

> *Well, let's start with what we're not. We are not the lad mag that caters to the 18-year-old man in the hunt. We're not the glossy fashion magazine that tells you that you need to have a pair of $3,000 shoes. We're not one of those magazines you have to hide from your wife or boss. We're something different, something real. We're what's been missing for real men.*[2]

Even the site's use of language is designed to resonate with dads.

Man of the House publishes one or two articles a day based on an editorial calendar. It also commissions outside experts to create content men enjoy. It has six primary expert contributors, plus guest writers who create the content for the site.

In nearly every case, these experts have already established an audience with dads. For example, Jason Avant, a featured contributor for Man of the House, is also founder of DadCentric.com, one of the leading blogs for dads.

Avant explained the mission of Man of the House: "The idea is to provide a magazine style Web site with stories that speak to today's 30- or 40-something dads, including how-to articles on how to manage your life."

Avant went on to say that Man of the House writers have a lot of leeway to write about what they want to. "The reason I like writing for Man of the House is because it's not an infomercial for P&G products," he said.

Man of the House has achieved an amazing degree of success in a very short period of time. *The keys to its explosive growth involved creating great content that was light on advertising and supported by experts.*

---

[2] See http://manofthehouse.com/about.

Although a billion-dollar company commissioned Man of the House, it has the feel of a much smaller site. And you don't need to be a megacorporation to achieve similar results for your business.

The beauty behind what P&G has pulled off is that it owns the platform. The company doesn't need to rely on middlemen or pay for costly advertising. Instead, it is growing something that will help the company connect with dads in a powerful way.

Let's assume you're not a huge corporation. Maybe you're even a one-person show. If that's the case, this next example is for you.

THE PIONEER WOMAN

Ree Drummond is a city girl who married a cowboy and moved to a cattle ranch in Oklahoma to start a family. Her passions include photography and cooking.

In 2006, she decided to start a blog to share pictures, recipes, and stories of her life living on the range. She called her site The Pioneer Woman (see ThePioneerWoman.com). What likely started as a hobby transformed Drummond into an Internet sensation and helped her become a *New York Times* best-selling author.

Drummond mixes her photography with creative writing to craft a visually stunning site designed to display the rural lifestyle for women (see Figure 6.2). She showcases cooking, photography, home and gardening, and home schooling. Her site is a solid case study in how to offer compelling content that is easy to read, visually appealing, and invites conversation.

With 22 million page views a month, Drummond is now connecting with a massive audience, and *Forbes* rated her as one of the top 25 Web celebrities in 2010—one of only three women to make the cut.

"People come and read one post, and then they send [a link] to their mom or their sister," said Drummond. "People can find something to relate to on the site, whether it's the food, or the ranch life, or photography."[3]

As a *Los Angeles Times* food columnist explains, "On the Pioneer Woman, a blog posting simply starts with a topic du jour and is followed up with photos and brief observations and interjections that

---

[3] Casserly, M. "Home On the Range with the Pioneer Woman," *Forbes*, March 3, 2010.

FIGURE 6.2 The Pioneer Woman site uses powerful visuals to connect with women.

Source: Reproduced by permission from Ree Drummond © January 5, 2011. PioneerWoman.com.

serve as captions. The effect invites readers to sit back, and lazily scroll through the photos, devouring and savoring each morsel as they go."[4]

Drummond also invites guest bloggers to contribute to the photography and home schooling portions of the site. And she started an online database called "The Tasty Kitchen," where her readers can submit and rank recipes.

In 2009, leveraging the success of her site, Drummond released her first book *The Pioneer Woman Cooks: Recipes from an Accidental Country Girl* (William Morrow Cookbooks), earning her the number-one slot on the *New York Times* bestseller list. Her latest book, also a best seller, is a memoir entitled *The Pioneer Woman: Black Heels to Tractor Wheels—A Love Story* (William Morrow, 2011).

Drummond treats readers of her site like friends. "The day I launched my cookbook, I was interviewed in Oklahoma at a book

---

[4] Lynch, R. "The Pioneer Woman, an Internet and publishing sensation," *Los Angeles Times*, September 23, 2009.

signing, and I felt like I was getting ready to meet 500 of my friends. That's the way the Internet is now—people connect to the world around all the time and make up these communities."[5]

Drummond has a very loyal base. "I love reading Pioneer Woman," said a fan. "She's a good writer, good photographer, and her life and outlook are both relatable and enviable. Her site is an escape, for sure, but also a bit of cheer."[6]

The Pioneer Woman has built a huge platform on top of outstanding content—content that generates instant affinity with women. Her bestselling books are an outcome of her platform, not what built it.

Drummond's site appears to be large and well established, despite being a one-woman show. It has almost no obvious marketing messages, and she's tapped into her base of readers to develop a comprehensive recipe database.

The Pioneer Woman is a pertinent example of how following a passion can often bring substantial rewards. With a platform much larger than many large traditional magazines, Drummond will likely be set for the rest of her life.

■ ■ ■

Both Man of the House and The Pioneer Woman have created something unique and highly relatable to their audiences. At the core of their success is great content.

What Makes for Great Content?

Great content is the first component of the elevation principle for a reason. Without it, all the experts and marketing in the world won't get your rocket ship very far. If you want to achieve significant growth, you must have content to fuel your marketing. And not just any content; you'll need outstanding content.

You know great content when you see it. But breaking down what goes into making great content is bit more complicated. To help get to the core of this question, I tapped SocialMediaExaminer.com's

---

[5] Casserly, M. "Home on the Range . . . ."
[6] Ibid.

active Facebook community, asking: "What makes content great? What separates great content from everything else?"

Here are some of the core elements of great content, direct from an active community of marketers:

Highly relevant: "For me, good content is relevant and targeted to its audience," said Carmen Portela. If your goal is to target dads, as Man of the House does, then creating content that is of great interest to many dads is essential.

To get to the core of what's relevant to people, you need to know them well. The more frequently you can deliver content that meets the needs and desires of a specific people group, the more relevant you will become to them. Always ask yourself, "Is this content relevant to my readers?"

Educational: If your Web site is dedicated to helping marketers learn how to employ social media tactics (like SocialMedia Examiner.com's mission), then your content should continue to deliver new ideas. Helping people discover new ways to solve common problems can quickly build you a loyal following.

"Great content speaks to the mind and heart of the reader—it empowers and catalyzes; it informs and inspires. Great content produces the aha! moment," said Roshan Khan.

Easy to digest: Highly relevant and educational content is irrelevant if you can't make it easy for people to understand. A conversational tone should be the basis for all of your content. "Connect the reader to something that makes sense in their world. Use metaphors, examples, or try comparing content to something from a popular movie or story," said Chrissanne Long.

Ryan Bokros adds, "Content must be pertinent to the topic, and stay on topic. There is no easier way to lose someone than to run down 10 different rabbit trails. I would rather see content that is shorter and to the point (while keeping the audience), than long, drawn out, and taking up a lot of space (while losing the audience)."

Visually appealing: The eye is just as important as the mind when it comes to readers. A visually attractive layout, like the content seen on The Pioneer Woman, can engage readers in a powerful way. The old saying, "A picture is worth a thousand words," is still alive and relevant.

Visuals go beyond images. Try to enhance your content with visual cues by **bolding key take-home messages** and *italicizing important terms*. Make sure your paragraphs are short. Use callouts and bullets to help the reader speed through your content.

Conversation inviting: "Great content isn't content. It's conversation. If you read what I'm writing and feel that I'm speaking to you—and of course you enjoy our 'conversation'—I have succeeded," said Farrukh Naeem. Conversational writing simply means writing like you speak.

If you want to connect with people, put aside your writing formalities. Your language doesn't need to be perfect. It's pretty simple to do. Simply speak out loud. Then write it all down.

Lacks a sales angle: "Avoid the hard sell; be the expert, not a salesperson," said Jen Hunt Walker. Great content shouldn't have any obvious marketing messages or sales pitches embedded inside of it.

If your content is about your specific product or service, that's not great content; it's marketing collateral. People won't flock to marketing materials.

In summary, great content must be relevant, educational, easy to read, and visually appealing; it also must invite conversation and lack any obvious marketing messages.

Let's take a look at a few different examples.

EXAMPLES OF GREAT CONTENT

This section contains two examples of great content. (Refer to the footnotes for links to the content for further study.)

The first example is from SocialMediaExaminer.com. Amy Porterfield, co-author (with Phyliss Khare and Andrea Vahl) of *Facebook Marketing All-in-One for Dummies* (For Dummies, 2011), crafted a post called "10 Top Facebook Pages and Why They're Successful."[7]

---

[7] See http: www.socialmediaexainer.com/top-10-facebook-pages.

Notice that this article opens with a few questions (see Figure 6.3). Porterfield asks: "Does your business have a Facebook page? Have you ever wondered what successful Facebook page owners are doing right?"

This simple mechanism allows her to connect with readers. If they can answer yes to the questions, they'll likely find the content relevant.

FIGURE 6.3 This is a good example of engaging content.

- ◆ *Key phrases are bolded.* To help accommodate the skim reader, key messages in the article are set in boldface. Such formatting makes it easy for readers to work through the article without missing important points.
- ◆ *Images are included.* Each of the 10 Facebook pages Porterfield references features multiple images to help the reader visualize why the page is successful.

Notice how popular the content is, charting more than 3,000 retweets. Because the purpose of this article is to showcase other successful Facebook pages, the readers of SocialMediaExaminer.com found outstanding value in the post.

Here's the second example:

Ree Drummond posted a recipe for chicken tortilla soup on her site, The Pioneer Woman (see Figure 6.4).[8] This post serves as an excellent yet simple example of great content. It is easy to read, visually appealing, and invites conversation.

The first thing readers see is a beautiful photograph demonstrating the outcome if they follow Drummond's instructions. Her photographs are very large. The full post actually contains a total of 37 original photographs.

But the power of this content goes way beyond the visuals. Drummond opens her post with the following content:

I love, love, love Chicken Tortilla Soup. So over the weekend, I made some.

The end.

Wasn't that a beautiful story?

Good! I'll tell you another one: Once upon a time there was a person.

That person was you. You made this soup. And you were happy.

The end.

∗Burp∗

Here's how you make it:

---

[8] See http://thepioneerwoman.com/cooking/2011/01/chicken-tortilla-soup.

Chicken Tortilla Soup

Posted by Ree in All PW Recipes, Cowgirl Food, PW's Favorites, Soups

JAN
10
2011

I love, love, love, love Chicken Tortilla Soup. So over the weekend, I made some.

The end.

Wasn't that a beautiful story?

Good! I'll tell you another one: Once upon a time there was a person. That person was you. You made this soup. And you were happy.

The end.

First, mix up some seasonings. This is cumin, chili powder, and garlic powder. I also stirred in some salt.

Figure 6.4   This example from The Pioneer Woman shows how strong visuals can help your content.

Source: Reproduced by permission from Ree Drummond © January 10, 2011. PioneerWoman.com.

This is a very powerful opening designed to resonate with Drummond's audience. Indeed, within mere hours of the article going live, she had 86 comments from her readers.

Notice how *Drummond uses simple stories to bring the reader into her life.* She also uses highly conversational language that her audience can relate to.

To test how well her content resonated with women, I asked my wife to have a look at the preceding article. Within two minutes, her response was, "I'm making this soup next week! Where did you find this?"

These two examples are a small sampling of thousands of outstanding articles that you could model for your readers. You just need to *start looking outside the box for great ideas.* (Be sure to reference the idea vault concept covered in Chapter 3.)

So far I've shown you some great content-based sites and examples. Now let's focus on *your* content. One of the first things you should think about is crafting an editorial guide.

Creating an Editorial Guide

An editorial guide is a reference that will help you and others produce outstanding content. An editorial guide is the instruction manual for mixing your rocket fuel for optimal performance.

Rather than suggesting you start from scratch, I'd like to provide you a sample.

SocialMediaExaminer.com's Editorial Guide

What follows was sourced from SocialMediaExaminer.com's editorial guide. Feel free to model your own guide along these very same lines.

> **Audience profile:** Please remember you are writing to a business audience who is *likely not very experienced with social media marketing* but is very knowledgeable about general marketing principles. Assume they understand some of the basic terms, like "tweet" and "retweet." Our reader is likely a *business owner* or *marketing professional. They are coming to Social Media Examiner to learn.*

> **Article length:** We suggest articles be at least 1,000 words in length (about two pages in Word). If your articles contain a lot of images, you can reduce the word count. However, content is key for us, so be sure to add plenty.

Use short sentences: Most online readers are skimmers. Accommodate them.

Add lots of subheads: Break your sections using **Bolded Subheads**. Try to get creative, as subheads lure readers to read your content.

Highlight key text: Please **bold**, or *italicize* key points you are trying to make. Feel free to mix the use as needed. Also, use bullets when you can.

Link to as many sources as possible: When you can, include a hotlink for any name, company, or quote so folks can go discover more. If you know how, please hotlink the actual words you want linked within Word. If you don't how to do this, simply follow this format: Mike Stelzner [link to http://twitter.com/mike_stelzner] is the founder of Social Media Examiner.

Use internal linking: Whenever possible, try to cross-reference at least one prior post residing on SocialMediaExaminer.com. Why? It helps our search engine optimization and also allows readers to dig deeper.

Try to quote people: Expert quotes always add to your work. You can source these from blogs, over e-mail, or over the phone.

Pictures: Please include at least one (ideally two) screenshots per article. Try to avoid clip art. Please try not to exceed 480 pixels wide for larger pictures and at least 280 pixels for smaller ones. If you do not know how to resize images, no problem—we'll do it. *Please also send over images separately so we can upload them to our server.*

Video: You may use video in your posts; however, we would prefer it to be in a supporting role. If you are entering your posts into WordPress, please let us format the video. Simply include the URL to the video.

End your article with engaging questions or an action request: To encourage discussion, always conclude your article with a question, such as "What are your thoughts?," "What's your experience?"; or an action request, such as, "Please enter your comments in the box below."

This guide contains details and pointers that help writers create engaging content. Because SocialMediaExaminer.com has more than 60 writers, the guide has been instrumental in ensuring people produce content that meets our standards.

Whenever new people want to write for our site, we vet their writing style and then send off our guide to ensure they understand what is expected of them.

I'd like to draw your attention to a few points from the preceding example:

Clearly identify your readers: Make sure your writers know whom they are writing for. This helps the writer think of this type of person when creating his or her content. If you'd like guidance on building a profile of your ideal readers, refer back to the "Whom Do You Want to Reach?" section in Chapter 3.

Content length: SocialMediaExaminer.com is a magazine-style Web site. Thus, our content is at least 1,000 words. Don't force that standard on yourself unless you also want to create a magazine-style site. Mashable.com, for example, averages only about 400 words per article. Pick a length of content that is ideal for your goals.

Content layout: Notice that the editorial guide contains a lot of stylistic direction when it comes to content presentation. This is an area that is often overlooked by businesses. Be sure your content is formatted in a visually attractive manner.

In the beginning, your style guide might be for an audience of one—*you*. Don't let that stop you from developing something that can guide your own creative process. As you grow and expand to include other contributing writers, you'll have something that can ensure their content meets your standards.

Once you have a guide that helps you connect your content with your readers, your next step is to create an editorial calendar.

Mapping an Editorial Calendar

In Chapter 2 I introduced the idea of putting your business on a trajectory (think of a space map), along with the concept of markers.

You may recall that markers are like space buoys on your space map—they guide you toward your goals.

Enter stage left, the editorial calendar. *An editorial calendar is your content publishing plan.* Typically used by traditional publishers, such a calendar allows you to step back and look at the topics your site will be publishing in the future. You can think of the content within your editorial calendar as markers.

For example, SocialMediaExaminer.com keeps a 60-day editorial calendar that contains the topic and author of every post we plan on publishing. This helps us make sure we're never too focused on a specific topic, and helps our writers submit their articles on a schedule.

Even if you're the sole writer for your company, an editorial calendar will ensure you're on a schedule to produce outstanding content.

The easiest way to craft an editorial calendar is to open up a spreadsheet and set dates. Inside each date you can include the name of the writer, the topic of the post, and when the article is due.

When you map out a few months into a calendar, you'll begin to see patterns emerge. Cindy King, managing editor of SocialMedia Examiner.com offered tips you should consider when creating your editorial calendar:

◆ *Pay attention to the days of the week.* Make sure your strongest articles for the week go out on days when there will be the most readers. In the case of SocialMediaExaminer.com, those days are Tuesdays and Thursdays.

◆ *Look for variety in categories.* If your site covers multiple categories of topics, don't overload any week with a single category. For example, having multiple articles on Facebook back to back may not be a good idea if Facebook is just one of many topics you cover.

◆ *Space out multiple authors.* If you have many different content contributors, you should consider evenly spacing out their pieces. Different authors have different styles and may attract special audiences. By spacing them out, you'll be sure to appeal to various sets of your reader base every day.

◆ *Be flexible.* Sometimes authors miss deadlines. Have a backup plan in place in case someone doesn't deliver. Other times you'll need to rearrange your editorial calendar to address breaking news.

Here's an example of a single week's editorial calendar from SocialMediaExaminer.com.

Monday, January 3
◆ Topic: New Year's predictions
◆ Title: "30 Social Media Predictions from 30 Social Media Pros"
◆ Author: Cindy King

Tuesday, January 4
◆ Topic: Research review
◆ Title: "The Top Social Media Tool for 2011 Is . . . "
◆ Author: Ruth M. Shipley

Wednesday, January 5
◆ Topic: Product review
◆ Title: "Is RockMelt the Social Web Browser of the Future?"
◆ Author: Elijah Young

Thursday, January 6
◆ Topic: LinkedIn, how-to
◆ Title: "5 Ways to Use LinkedIn Groups to Build Influential Connections"
◆ Author: Stephanie Sammons

Friday, January 7
◆ Topic: Tools
◆ Title: "What Your Business Needs to Know about Social Graphs"
◆ Author: Jeff Korhan

Saturday, January 8
◆ Topic: News
◆ Title: "8 Social Media News Items You Need to Know"
◆ Author: Cindy King

As you can see, we spaced out the types of content we publish to appeal to different subsets of our reader base.

Think about your editorial calendar. What topics should you write about, and when? Who should write them? Spend time coming up with a calendar. Constantly update and refine it.

Why Content?

People love to discover new ideas that can help them improve themselves or their businesses. Great free content—designed to provide your ideal readers precisely what they seek—is highly valuable to people. It's a gift.

The content you steadily produce becomes a powerful fuel to help you grow a massive audience. That very same fuel will quickly take your rocket ship to new places as your reader base consumes it with great enthusiasm.

As the examples in this chapter demonstrate, great content must be relevant, should educate, and needs to be easy to read and visually appealing while inviting conversation. And there must be no obvious traces of marketing messages.

When you make producing incredible content the core of your marketing efforts, you'll stand apart from your competitors, who are spending fortunes advertising on other people's platforms. Not only will you be developing an online property you can call your own, you'll also inspire a raving fan base that will help you grow your business.

I encourage you to closely study sites that create outstanding content. Watch how they compose their content and track the response of their readers. Then begin applying what you've learned to your own business.

■ ■ ■

This chapter laid a foundation for the importance of great content. Through a series of examples, you've discovered how other successful businesses are using content.

You also now know what the core elements of good content are and the importance of an editorial guide. You've also discovered how an editorial calendar can help you develop the right mix of content for your reader base.

You should now begin thinking about the type of content you can publish on your own site.

In the next chapter I will show you how to create primary fuel—regular content that will attract a large base to your business.

Creating and Using Primary Fuel

Do not wait to strike till the iron is hot; but make it hot by striking.
—William Butler Yeats

The right content has the power to shape opinions, change minds, and spur action. It also fuels your business, propelling your rocket ship through the atmosphere toward new frontiers.

The sky isn't your limit. The moon is only your rest stop. Great content will take you to far-off star systems and unimaginable destinations.

Much like gasoline fuels your car, primary fuel powers your business; it's the regular content you need to move your rocket ship. In your car, you might be able to go a week on a single tank of gas. But once you run out, your ride is nothing more than a useless three-ton hunk of steel and iron. In the same way, without primary fuel your business won't go anywhere.

Primary fuel propels your business. It's fuel that's consumed by your reader base. It has a shelf life and must be replenished. And no, you can't fill up on it at the local gas station.

In this chapter I will examine the importance of creating primary fuel, and look at what it can achieve. I'll also provide details on how to create the six different types of primary fuel.

What Is Primary Fuel?

I mentioned in Chapter 1 that I have daughters, and explained that there are two ways to get their hair brushed. Yelling, "Get your behind over here, right now!" is one option. The other is to walk alongside them, brushing as they go on their merry way. I then applied this metaphor to businesses.

Too often we treat our customers (and prospects) like children. We scream at them with our advertising, try to intercept them as they run their lives, and get angry when they don't act on our commands.

As parents, the day ultimately comes when we realize we can't control what our children decide to do. As a marketer or business owner, that day *has* come: *You no longer hold sway or influence over your customers.* A wise person once told me, "They're gonna do what they're gonna do."

What's the solution? Rather than impose your will on people, simply walk alongside them. And that's precisely the power of primary fuel.

Primary fuel is regularly produced free content that meets the needs of your reader base. Typically created in written form, primary fuel feeds your ideal base in the form of valuable articles, expert interviews, reviews, and more.

Primary fuel becomes the core of your marketing. Rather than placing costly ads on other people's properties, this type of content is something you create—and it helps you build your own platform.

The easiest way to use primary fuel is through blogging. However, your fuel can reach people in many different venues. For example, e-mail newsletters, YouTube videos, and podcasts are all possible channels where you can "burn" primary fuel.

The ideal situation is to create content on your own platform (like your blog), but that's not necessarily a requirement. You may find producing content for other, larger, publications is just as valuable to your business. The key is to regularly generate primary fuel and make sure your ideal base is consuming it.

WHY DOES PRIMARY FUEL WORK?

In Chapter 5 I talked about the power of giving gifts. When you give people gifts they really want, they'll be drawn to you and your business.

Similarly, getting their problems solved is a universal need for most people. *If you can help your reader base solve their problems with your free content, they'll become raving fans.* This is the goal of primary fuel.

Here's an example: Think of a business consultancy that helps business owners get organized. I'll call the firm Get Your Life Back. Let's say this company started producing regular tips that business owners find valuable.

Perhaps one article offered advice on how to clear your desk by the end of each workday, and the next included tips on scheduling your time. What if Get Your Life Back began doing interviews with experts like David Allen, author of *Getting Things Done: The Art of Stress-Free Productivity* (Penguin, 2002)? What if it began reviewing all the new books on topics like getting your business organized, managing stress, and selling?

If Get Your Life Back became known as a reliable source of insight—due to its regularly published content—it would quickly grow a large following. It would become an indispensable resource for business owners—a trusted source. And if that happened, the firm would experience massive growth and sales.

Why? Because Get Your Life Back would no longer need to hunt for prospects. Rather, its ideal customers would be regularly consuming its content and referring others. Its Web site would become a gathering ground for a large community of ideal prospects. And, likely, many would become paying customers.

This is the model that SocialMediaExaminer.com follows. We publish daily articles that help marketers grow their businesses with social media. We carefully mix how-to posts, expert interviews, case studies, reviews, and news designed for marketers.

It doesn't matter whether your ideal reader base is consumers or business professionals. As long as you empower them with primary fuel, they'll take your business places.

Here are some reasons why making primary fuel is *essential* for your business:

People will keep coming back: When you become known for publishing great content that meets the desires of your reader base, they'll frequently visit your site and seek out your content.

This is better than any advertising investment. When people make consuming your content a regular part of their life, you'll gain something that money can't buy.

Your content will be recommended: As you produce outstanding content, people will tell their friends and peers. When your ideal base begins evangelizing your content, you'll become highly valuable to them. Those recommendations to others are priceless for your business. They'll help you quickly expand your base.

Some people will want to help you: People in your base will reach out to help you, unsolicited! For example, some will choose to provide you valuable feedback, to improve your content; others will help you promote your paid products; and still others will offer their services at no cost. Often the response will be something like this: "I love what you're doing and have found so much value from it! How can I help you?"

You'll be perceived as an authoritative source: When you produce valuable content on a regular basis, your base will listen to what you have to say. You'll have earned their trust. When you're classified in their mind as an authority, it will lead to opportunities to speak to their groups, join panel discussions, and participate in exclusive business ventures.

You'll inspire deep loyalty: As you become known for your great content, your base will begin to group together as loyal fans. When you need feedback or help, many will leap forward to assist, without hesitation. When you attend events, they'll come to meet you. Much like movie stars have fans, you'll have a raving fan base that greatly values your ideas and time.

Experts will be willing to work with you: As your content begins earning a reputation for your business, experts will become aware of you. Some will approach you and want to participate. Others will immediately say yes to your requests to interview them. It will become easy to work with power players in your industry.

When you decide to sell something, readers will buy it: Once you've established valuable equity with your reader base, many will consider what you have to sell. In fact, the common barriers to selling will be broken down because you will have become a known and trusted source. This is perhaps one of the most important reasons to make creating primary fuel central to your marketing strategy.

Now that you're sold on the value of primary fuel, the next question is, how does it work?

How Does Primary Fuel Work?

The benefits of using primary fuel are amazing and numerous. But how does it actually work?

Primary fuel gives people a reason to keep coming back to you. For example, popular musicians know they need to keep releasing new albums to maintain their popularity. Television networks know they need to keep creating new shows to compete. Magazines must put out new issues each week or month.

Thanks to the Web, you are the music company, the television network, and the magazine—you're a publisher when you use primary fuel. The Internet is your distribution channel. Your fans are your readers.

You no longer need to rely on costly distribution networks. The Web makes it easy for you to produce and deliver content that others want. You simply need to make it and publish it.

Here are the basic steps for creating and using primary fuel:

Step 1: Produce the fuel. When mixing primary fuel, you need a few key ingredients. You'll start with some great content (more on that in a bit). Then it needs to be tailored to meet the needs of your ideal base.

Step 2: Process the fuel. Once you've got something that can work as primary fuel, the next step is to have it processed by someone else. This person could be an editor or a peer. They'll check to make sure there are no "impurities" in your content (like typos or inappropriate marketing messages).

Step 3: Release the fuel. Once the fuel has been purified, it's ready for consumption by your reader base. You can deliver the fuel to your blog or someone else's site. As people consume the fuel, it will start burning off over a period of days. The typical shelf life of primary fuel is 72 hours.

Step 4: Repeat the process. To keep your rocket ship moving forward, you'll need to produce more fuel and start the process again.

I don't want you to freak out about the idea of regularly producing primary fuel. Keep in mind that no business achieves success by sitting back and waiting for someone else to do something. *The reason so many of the businesses showcased in this book are thriving is precisely because they understand the importance of becoming a publisher.*

Rather than burning dollars on complex advertising campaigns, the elevation principle represents a marketing paradigm shift. When you start looking at content creation as a marketing investment, you'll begin to justify the effort involved.

WHO SHOULD CREATE YOUR CONTENT?

Whether you're working from a spare room in your house or a cubicle inside a corporation, *you can do this.* The good news is you don't need to go it alone.

There are a few options to consider when deciding *who should create your content.* As I see it, there are four possible pools of people to draw from when creating primary fuel:

1. *You:* It really should start with you. If you can write or conduct interviews, then you should be a primary source of content for your business. You don't need to be the sole source, however. In the case of SocialMediaExaminer.com, I contribute about three times a month—usually in the form of video interviews. Those interviews are very easy for me to do, and I enjoy meeting experts in person.

2. *Outside experts:* If you can persuade experts outside of your business to create content for you, you'll be off and running quickly. They'll provide credibility and outstanding content, a win-win situation. (Review the section in Chapter 4 on finding

experts for more on this.) The ideal situation is to find an expert to contribute an article a month. You'll likely need many experts to fill your editorial calendar.

3. *Employees:* If you have people working at your company who can write or conduct interviews, you'll want to encourage them to join your content team. Southwest Airlines has a number of employees who regularly blog on the BlogSouthwest.com site. A side benefit is that employees will likely find creating content a fun alternative to their daily tasks.

4. *Freelance writers:* With so many traditional journalists out of work these days, you won't have to look far to find freelance writers you can hire to help you create content. One good source is Elance.com, which has a huge marketplace for freelance writers. If you're looking for a more refined list of writers, check out Junta42.com or MediaBistro.com. In most cases, you'll be able to justify the investment in free-lancers as a marketing expense. Think about it this way: If you have employees writing for you (or if you're doing it yourself), that is actually *costing* your business. By using freelancers, you'll be working with professional writers at a very afford-able rate.

Creating primary fuel doesn't need to be difficult, and frankly can be very fun. You might be wondering what primary fuel looks like.

SIX TYPES OF PRIMARY FUEL

There are six types of powerful primary fuel you can regularly produce for your business. I suggest you mix up the types of fuel you use, because your reader base might get bored consuming only one type of content on a regular basis, and drop off. When you vary your use of primary fuel, you will also engage different subsets of your reader base. Just keep in mind that some forms are harder to create than others.

It's worth noting that the six types of fuel I describe here are not the only options available to you. They're the ones we've found to be highly effective. We've experimented with other, more "offbeat" types of fuel, like custom cartoons, but found they just didn't generate the kind of response for us these six types do.

The six types of primary fuel that have proven effective for SocialMediaExaminer.com are:

◆ How-to articles
◆ Expert interviews
◆ Reviews
◆ Case studies
◆ News stories
◆ Contrarian stories

Throughout the rest of this chapter I'll demonstrate what goes into creating each of these types of fuel.

Comprehensive How-to Articles

The bread and butter of your content should be *articles that explain to your reader base how to overcome important challenges they face.* This type of content is popular because it meets the needs of your readers. When people discover something new, they'll find great value in your content, pushing your rocket ship further out into space.

To create great how-to articles, *you need to know your readers' hot button issues.* (Refer back to the section in Chapter 4 on determining the desires of your ideal reader base.) When you hit a chord with people, they will widely share and reference your articles.

In the case of SocialMediaExaminer.com, nearly half of all of our published articles focus on how to use social media to grow a business. We carefully examine the latest trends in our marketplace and recruit writers to author comprehensive articles on relevant topics.

For example, when Foursquare was growing in popularity, we produced a number of articles on how to use the geolocation service to drive traffic to local businesses.

Here are some of the titles of those articles:

◆ "Foursquare: Are You Checking Out the Hottest Social Media App?"
◆ "Why Foursquare Drives Business: What You Need to Know"
◆ "How to Drive More Customers to Your Local Business with Social Geotagging"

Take a look at the example how-to article in Appendix A called "How to Use Twitter to Grow Your Business." This particular piece was very popular. As you read it, pay close attention to how experts are cited to support the key points of the article.

You might be wondering, what's the structure of how-to articles?

THE COMPONENTS OF HOW-TO ARTICLES

How-to articles are usually beefy pieces that contain at least 1,000 words. If you don't have significant substance in your article, people won't find it as valuable as it should be.

Here are the *core elements of a how-to piece*:

Opening Statement Connect with your readers by asking a few questions they can relate to. For example, if you're writing an article on how to discipline children, you might start with an opening like this: "Are your kids out of control? Do you wish they'd listen to you? If so, look no further. This article will reveal proven techniques from parents just like you."

Setting the Stage Here's where you define critical terms and explain why the reader should even care. This component of how-to articles is often overlooked.

When you set the stage with readers, you properly align them with your content. Your opening statement may have grabbed the readers, but you still need to give them reasons why they should keep reading your article.

Continuing with the disciplining children example, let me show you what I mean:

> *Perhaps you grew up with a strict parent and vowed never to be so stiff with your children. Or maybe you're concerned that if you punish your kids they'll love you less. Studies show that children who lack discipline often struggle later in life. You know you need to do something different . . .*

You can see how this paragraph is designed to address some common concerns parents face, while connecting with them at the same time. If I were a parenting expert (and I'm not), I might go on to explain how out-of-control kids impact marriages, classroom experiences, and so on.

The point here is to simply write a few paragraphs that explain why the reader needs to pay attention to the article. The goal is to build some affinity with the reader, so he or she thinks, "Yes, that's precisely why I need to do something about this. I want to learn how."

The opening statement and setting the stage components are often used in persuasive sales letters and landing pages. Frequently, the how-to details are reserved as special content available only to people who purchase a product or event. That's why, when you proceed to *deliver the how-to solution for free, you'll set your content apart.*

Once you've properly set the stage, your article is ready to describe the solution to the problem.

Revealing the How-to Details   At this point in your article, you should explain to your readers how they can solve their problem.

Should You Give Your Knowledge Away for Free?

If you make your living selling knowledge, you might be resistant to sharing how-to details for free. Here are a few thoughts for you.

When my primary business was writing white papers for companies, I shared extensive how-to details in free articles. I knew doing so enabled some of my readers to create their own white papers. At the same time, it demonstrated my expertise to those people who didn't have the time to try it themselves.

I also never revealed certain aspects of the process for free. For example, I rarely wrote about how to create the core components of a white paper in my articles (I reserved those details for my book and courses). Instead, I focused my free content on how to market with white papers, how to write headlines, and how to connect with readers.

So you might want to consider taking a "useful but incomplete" approach to your how-to articles. This means you provide valuable insight, but not share everything you know. And even if you do reveal all you know, you'll still find most people can't do it the way you do. But the response from your reader base will be enormous, as you share details never made freely available before.

Often, the best how-to articles reveal a number of tips. For example:

What follows are five easy ways to get your children to stop their disobedient behavior and listen to you.

The rest of this article would provide plenty of details, crafted in a manner that is easy to understand.

The details portion of how-to articles can be arranged in a number of different ways, including:

- *Step-by-step:* If there's a logical progression of steps your readers should take to accomplish the goal of the article, then outlining those steps should be the core of your article. For example, if you were writing an article about how to register your business on Foursquare, this might be an ideal approach.
- *X-number of tips/ways:* Itemizing a number of tips or ways to solve a problem is another popular approach. For example, we published an article on SocialMediaExaminer.com called, "26 Tips to Enhance Your Experience on LinkedIn." If you can support some of your tips with images, such as screenshots or stock photography, it will further enhance the article.
- *X-number of examples:* Sometimes, providing examples of others who are doing it right is more than sufficient. For example, "10 Top Facebook Pages and Why They're Successful" was an article published by SocialMediaExaminer.com.

Be sure to study the sample in Appendix A, or take a look at the how-to category on SocialMediaExaminer.com for models.

Enhancing Your Content with Images

Your content must capture the eyes of your readers before it can capture their minds. Images can help convey your message in a powerful way. Ideally, you should have an image for every 300 words.

Avoid using cheesy clip art in your articles. Instead, try to rely on screenshots and stock photography. For example, if you are writing a post about how to use an online service, support it with screen captures and captions. Alternatively, if you are writing about a concept, like parenting, consider photographs.

Here are a few reliable sources for finding photographic images to use in your content:

Flickr.com: Conduct an advanced search on this site. Be sure to check the box that refers to using only Creative-Commons content; this will ensure you don't violate any copyrights when placing images on your site. You'll need to link back to the source of the image in your article. This is typically done in the caption or at the bottom of your article.

iStockPhoto.com: This site contains a massive repository of professional images of very high quality. You pay a small fee for credits, which can be used to purchase images and vector-based illustrations.

ShutterStock.com: This site is similar to iStockPhoto, and worth checking out.

Expert Interviews

Conducting interviews with experts is a core component of the elevation principle. Great content plus other people is what helps your business grow quickly. Part of the "other people" component is content that results from expert interviews.

When you interview people who have professional knowledge in topical areas of interest to your ideal base, *you'll be able to easily generate outstanding content and build relationships with experts.* (Refer to Chapter 3, the section on discovering people, for more on how to find experts, and to Chapter 4, the section on working with outside experts, to learn how to persuade them to participate.)

Keep in mind that the most approachable experts have typically authored books or work for businesses that are known in your industry.

SocialMediaExaminer.com regularly interviews experts in the fields of marketing and social media. We publish at least three interviews a month. For example, I conducted an interview with Frank Eliason, senior vice president of social media at Citigroup, titled, "Why Social Media Is Inseparable from Customer Service."

In this interview, with Frank on camera, I asked him about his thoughts on the current state of customer service and social media (see Figure 7.1).

You also should check out the written interview example in Appendix B called, "How to Succeed with Social Media: A Brian Solis Interview." Take a look at the type of questions I asked and note the flow of the interview.

FIGURE 7.1   Here I'm introducing Frank Eliason at a major trade show.

THE COMPONENTS OF EXPERT INTERVIEWS

Expert interviews can take place in many different formats. You can interview an expert over the phone and have it transcribed into an article or produced as an audio podcast. Alternatively, you can conduct video interviews.

If you want to do video interviews, be sure to check out Steve Garfield's excellent book, *Get Seen: Online Video Secrets to Building Your Business* (Wiley, 2010). Also watch Social Media Examiner TV's episode, "How to Integrate Video into Your Social Media Marketing" at SocialMediaExaminer.com.

Carefully weigh the pros and cons of all four types of interviews: written, audio, video, and hybrid. Decide if one or more is right for your business.

Written interviews: This type of interview has strong search engine optimization advantages, and can easily accommodate skim-readers. However, some production work is required to create written interviews. Typically, you'll need to transcribe a recorded interview and then trim it down to a more digestible size. You'll also need to add support images.

Audio interviews: These are very easy to create. You simply record the interview and post it on your site. The downside to audio interviews is that they are linear, meaning people can't skim them. If the interview is not strong, people will likely drop off.

Video interviews: Video can be very easy to produce using a simple portable video camera. Being able to see experts adds a personal touch to your interviews for viewers. However, video interviews can be a major production, as they involve special lighting, power, microphones, camera equipment, software, and videographers. And, like audio, video is a linear medium, thus the content needs to be well polished or you'll lose viewers. Editing video is also very time-consuming.

Hybrid interviews: Consider mixing formats. At SocialMedia Examiner.com, we mix formats in every one of our interviews. For example, when we do an audio interview, we transcribe it and make an article out of the best portions of it. We then include a link to the full audio interview. When we conduct on-camera interviews, we always pull out the key messages from the video and insert them into our post. (For an excellent example of combining video and text, see David Garland's expert interviews at TheRiseToTheTop.com.)

No matter which format you choose, expert interviews require preparation and effort. However, the rewards are well worth it, often resulting in outstanding content.

Here are a few tips for conducting an expert interview:

◆ *Tell the expert who your audience is.* Explain who will be watching, listening, or reading the final interview. For example, "Our audience comprises mostly marketers and business owners who are just getting started with social media." This helps the expert frame his or her answers and ensures a better interview for your ideal base.

◆ *Explain the format.* Tell your expert what will occur during the interview and what they can expect. When I am doing a telephone interview, I'll share that I plan to ask questions for about 30 minutes. I also suggest to experts that they take their time answering questions, and alert them that I may dig deeper with follow-on questions.

◆ *Go over the questions you plan on asking.* At the start of the interview share with the expert the precise questions you'd like to ask. This allows you to modify or remove questions the expert doesn't feel comfortable answering.

◆ *Confirm the expert's biography.* Read out loud to the expert how you plan on introducing him or her. This will allow you to correct job titles and name pronunciation, if necessary. It also ensures that you've highlighted the key accomplishments the expert wants mentioned.

◆ *Keep it conversational.* The best interviews come across as two people "just talking." If the expert says something that spurs an idea, feel free to go off-script and ask follow-on questions.

◆ *Explain the publication process.* Once the interview is complete, explain what you'll be doing with the material and when the expert can expect to see it. Offer to contact him or her when the interview goes live.

Now here are some *mistakes you should avoid*, which I learned firsthand:

- *Don't pitch your business.* Remember that the interview should be perceived as a gift to the expert (review the section on gifts in Chapter 5). So avoid talking about your business in any level of detail. Reframe your thinking: The interview is you creating great content for your audience, not an opportunity to sell to the expert.
- *Don't talk "over" the expert.* Let the expert be the expert. This means let the conversation happen naturally. Your goal is to guide the discussion, ensuring the best content comes from the mouth of your expert. Don't try to be the expert yourself; instead, make sure the spotlight is shining fully on your guest.
- *Don't ask for any favors.* Try your best *not* to employ the rule of reciprocity. This means don't ask the expert to share the interview with his or her fans; don't ask the expert to help you; *don't ask for anything.* Realize the value of the interview and the expert's time is a favor that's already been given to you.

Here are some questions you can use over and over again in expert interviews:

What is X? This type of question simply asks the expert to explain something he or she is intimately familiar with. For example, if you are interviewing someone who has written a book, you could say something like this: "Jeff Hazlett, what exactly is *The Mirror Test?*" This was my opening question to Hazlett, the former CMO of Kodak. These types of questions are easy for the expert to explain.

How does X impact Y? This type of question takes a topic (like social media) and asks how it affects a product, group, or industry. For example, when I interviewed Scott Monty from Ford, I asked, "How has social media impacted the release of your new cars?" When I interviewed Mark Burnett, executive producer of the hit TV show *Survivor*, I asked, "How will social media tools like Twitter and Facebook have an impact on people's viewership of reality television?"

How have things changed? Often, experts are on the leading edge of their markets. Simply by asking what has changed, typically you'll get an interesting and introspective answer. For example, in an interview with Darren Rowse, author of *ProBlogger*, I asked "How has blogging changed in the last 12 months, and why?"

What trends are you seeing? Asking an expert to describe what he or she sees as industry trends can often result in some really interesting discussions. For example, when I interviewed Rohit Bhargava, author of *Personality Not Included: Why Companies Lose Their Authenticity and How Great Brands Get It Back* (McGraw-Hill, 2008), I asked, "What are the trends that big businesses should be paying attention to?"

What advice or tips would you give your peers? If you're interviewing an expert who has a strong track record of success in your industry, consider asking him or her for tips or advice for others who are struggling to achieve similar success. I asked Chris Brogan, co-author (with Julien Smith), of *Trust Agents: Using the Web to Build Influence, Improve Reputation, and Earn Trust* (Wiley, 2009), "For businesses and marketers that are not deep into social media, where should they get started with social media?"

Be sure to study the sample in Appendix B, and take a look at the expert interviews available on SocialMediaExaminer.com for models.

Reviews

When you review other people's books, products, or services, you accomplish two things: First, when you create a review, you provide *highly valuable content to your reader base in the form of an objective opinion.* When you direct a critical eye to something your audience might want to purchase, revealing the pros and cons, you become a trusted resource, one they know they can count on to help them make decisions.

The second advantage to doing reviews is often overlooked: When you review a book or a company's products, you'll likely *get the attention of the author or company.* This is especially true in the case of book reviews. When you place an honest assessment of authors' work up for public consumption, you gain a major opportunity to give a gift to high-profile individuals. This could become a foot in the door to working with an expert down the road.

Sometimes people will ask you for reviews. For example, SocialMediaExaminer.com does a monthly book review that has become highly coveted by book authors. Because we only review 12 books a year—and dozens come out related to social media annually—we're rather picky about the books we review. We've become known for our reviews. Authors come out of the woodwork trying to get a review from us. Many of these experts later turn out to work with us in other capacities.

In addition, we also regularly review new social media tools, providing detailed assessments. Our reader base loves reviews because they help them determine where to focus their limited time and attention.

Think about your industry. Which books, products, Web sites, or businesses could you review? Would your audience appreciate an objective analysis of them?

For an example of an excellent book review, be sure to check out the review example in Appendix C called, "The Secrets of YouTube Marketing Revealed," by Ruth Shipley. Carefully analyze how this review was crafted. You'll notice at first glance that it doesn't appear to be a book review at all. I'll explain more about that in a bit.

THE COMPONENTS OF REVIEWS

Reviews can take place in different formats. You can write reviews as articles or record them as videos. Alternatively, you can add a video review to an article.

Here are a few notes on videos:

If you're reviewing a Web site or online service, you should consider investing in software that allows you to actually show people what you are reviewing. This is called *screencasting* software because it captures everything shown on your screen as you do your review (along with your audio).

For example, Elijah R. Young wrote a review titled "Is RockMelt the Social Web Browser of the Future?" for SocialMediaExaminer.com.

He recorded a seven-minute video showing people how the Web browser worked, and added his opinions about RockMelt.

Recording this type of video review is easy—if you have the right software. If you're on a Mac, I highly recommend ScreenFlow. If you're on a Windows machine, Camtasia is a terrific solution.

Book reviews can also be done via video. Showing yourself on camera holding and talking about a book can be a powerful yet simple way to present a review.

For example, I decided to do a video review of David Meerman Scott's book *Real-Time Marketing & PR: How to Instantly Engage Your Market, Connect with Customers, and Create Products That Grow Your Business Now* (Wiley, 2010). While sitting in my office, I spoke simply about why I liked the book, as you can see in Figure 7.2.

You can also upload the video to Amazon.com as a video review of an author's book.

Here are a few tips to consider when doing a review:

Be Honest   Don't try to score points by kissing up to an author or company when you don't really believe the product is outstanding. Your readers will respect you more if you provide a true assessment of the strengths and shortcomings of whatever you review.

FIGURE 7.2   Here I am doing a video review of David Meerman Scott's book *Real-Time Marketing & PR*.

An honest, critical viewpoint is more respected by authors, as well. For example, "While I wish Michael Stelzner included more examples of businesses applying his model, I still think *Launch* is an outstanding book for any business."

Include Images   When you write your review, it's a good idea to add supporting images to strengthen the visual appeal of your article. If you're reviewing a book, try to get the cover image of the book and a photo of the author. If you're reviewing an online product or Web site, take some screenshots and add them to your review.

Add Tips and Other Details   Whether you're doing a product review or a book review, be sure to make suggestions to your reader base. In the case of a book, you could pull a few tips from the book and paraphrase them in your article. If it's a product review, you might want to provide some pointers from your experience using the product.

Rank the Review   Consider coming up with a standard ranking system that people can use to judge your final assessments. For example, SocialMediaExaminer.com uses a five-star system to rate books.

Alternative Reviews   You might want to consider *variations on straight reviews.* Here are two alternatives to the traditional review:

◆ *Article review:* Rather than titling your post simply "Book Review: Launch," consider making your review into an actual article that would be highly valuable to your readers. This type of review is really an article with an embedded book review.

    For example, you could create one titled, "10 Types of Content That Grow Your Business," and proceed to outline the content types discussed in this very book. Deeper into the article you could reveal the title of book and your thoughts on it. This is a viable alternative to a traditional book review because you are providing valuable insight to your reader base and suggesting a book they should consider to learn more. The example in Appendix C is this type of review.

♦ *Expert interview review:* If you want phone time with a high-profile author, set up an interview and then be sure to talk about the book at some point during the interview. This is similar to the model employed by talk-show hosts who have movie stars on their shows. Those stars show up as long as they know they will be given a chance to talk about their latest movie.

Turn back to the expert interview section a few pages earlier to see how to do such an interview. That said, make sure to source at least a few questions from the expert's new book during the interview.

♦ *Research Reviews:* If your business covers a unique industry or niche, you might want to review the latest research studies as they come out. This involves writing about the key highlights of reports. Your audience will often use these research findings to justify their activities or purchases.

Visit SocialMediaExaminer.com and click on the research category to see how we create these types of reviews. Also, be sure to study the sample in Appendix C, or take a look at the reviews on SocialMediaExaminer.com for models.

Case Studies

Creating case studies about other businesses in your industry is a powerful form of content.

♦ First, case studies satisfy the "other people" component of the elevation principle. When you showcase successful businesses, highlighting what they do right, you offer encouragement to your reader base.

♦ Second, case studies simply make for great content. When your readers read how others are winning, they'll discover new ideas or tips that could help them achieve success.

♦ Third, you can form stronger ties with showcased businesses, which could lead to future partnerships.

♦ Finally, this type of content can be a lot of fun to create.

A case study is an examination of a successful business or individual. This type of story often details the challenges people faced, what they did to overcome those challenges, and the actual results they achieved.

You might be thinking you could use case studies to showcase your customers. That's not what I'm suggesting here.

If you want outstanding content, seek case studies that have *absolutely no connection to your products, services, or clients*. Rather, look for an outstanding story that will encourage and empower your reader base. If you treat a case study as a powerful content tool—*not* a marketing tool—you'll find people will welcome it with open arms.

For example, let's say you sell software that helps businesses manage their employees and your objective is to build a destination for human resource professionals. If you focus on businesses using your software, your Web site will look like one big marketing brochure to your reader base.

Instead, find interesting and thought-provoking stories of thriving businesses and, simply, share their stories—whether they use your software or not. You never need to mention the precise software investment by name, just tell their story.

When you share compelling success stories, *you'll be perceived as a journalist, not a marketer*. This is important from two angles: First, the company you want to showcase will likely agree if you are perceived as a press opportunity. Second, your audience will respond favorably to your story.

Here's an example of how a case study might look.

SocialMediaExaminer.com published a piece called "How Social Media Helped Cisco Shave $100,000+ Off a Product Launch." Case study expert Casey Hibbard (author of *Stories That Sell: Turn Satisfied Customers into Your Most Powerful Sales & Marketing Asset*; AIM Publishers, 2009), created the story. (See Appendix D for the Cisco success story.)

Casey interviewed LaSandra Brill from Cisco for the story, which detailed how the company was able to save significant amounts of money by employing low-cost social media product launch tactics.

The resulting article was very popular on our site. And once it went live, LaSandra added to the story by replying to questions from our readers. We later recruited her to speak at one of our summits.

As you can see, case studies can be powerful from multiple dimensions, providing not only excellent content but partnership opportunities, as well.

What goes into making a successful case study?

THE COMPONENTS OF CASE STUDIES

If you decide to produce case studies, I strongly advise you to pick up a copy of Casey Hibbard's book, *Stories That Sell*.

Before I share the core components of case studies, let me answer a question you might be asking: *"Where do I find candidates for success stories?"* Here are a few tips to get you started:

- *Ask your reader base*. Tap the collective knowledge of your reader base. For example, "Which businesses do you think are best leveraging Facebook marketing, and why?" I've asked this very question. The resulting responses from your questions will allow you to discover businesses doing innovative things.
- *Read other publications*. The ideal situation, of course, is to break a new story, but there's nothing wrong with finding candidates from your publisher peers. Simply reach out to the company for an interview and retell its success story in your own words.
- *Keep your eyes and ears open at events*. If you're at an event and see a first-rate presentation from a potential candidate, consider doing a case study. Often, event coordinators seek people with pertinent case studies to share. Events can often be the source of important discoveries.
- *Watch for opportunities*. I received an e-mail from someone working for World Wrestling Entertainment (WWE), providing me some feedback. I responded via e-mail, asking him questions about what WWE was doing. That ultimately led to a very interesting case study.

Once you have a candidate locked down, here's what goes into the creation of a case study:

The challenge: To make your story strong, you need to start with a little history and provide some context. Explain why the business decided it needed to change. What were the problems that forced it to seek a new solution? When you write about the company's problems, you'll help your readers identify with the story.

In the Cisco example in Appendix D, the company was spending a fortune on product launches. It saw the allure of social media as a possible lower-cost alternative.

Solution steps taken: What did the company do to overcome its problems? Be precise and share its experiences. This is the section that your reader base will find the most interesting. The Cisco article described nine different social tactics the company employed.

The results: Share the results achieved by the company profiled in your case study. This is where numbers are important. How much did the company earn or save? Be as specific as the showcased company will allow. Results speak loudly to your reader base, and will often be used as justification for someone trying a similar tactic.

Quotations: Ideally, you'll be recording an interview in preparation for your case study. You'll want to grab key "soundbites" from the source. Peppering the story with quotes from the spokesperson adds a human element to the story.

Lessons learned: You also might want to ask the case study subject for tips or pointers he or she can share with your readers. These often make powerful supporting material for your case study.

Be sure to study the Cisco example in Appendix D, and take a look at the case studies on SocialMediaExaminer.com for models.

News Stories

I could have just as easily titled this section, "What's New." If your industry is in constant flux or experiencing growth, you should consider covering news. *News stories are the latest industry developments that would interest your readers.*

Think about the types of stories you read on large online news sites. For example, when I was writing this book, Facebook was a major source of news in the social media world. Each time the company announced a new capability or feature, my audience wanted to know the details.

Before going any further here, I should warn you that *covering news could be a difficult proposition.*

If you break news stories, your site could receive a massive influx of traffic. However, there are numerous downsides to making news stories one of your main sources of content.

◆ First, you'll always be racing to be the first to cover a story. Typically, the goal is to release a story before it goes mainstream. This often means prioritizing speed over quality of content. Depending on how much is changing in your industry, you could find yourself burning out pretty quickly.

◆ Second, your articles become old news almost immediately. This means your Web site will always be "living for the moment," and rarely will older content be of any value to people visiting your site for the first time. No one cares about old news. This means you'll attract an audience that wants to keep up, but only as long as you can remain the best source for news.

◆ Third, you'll likely be inundated by requests from companies wanting you to write about what they think is news. Speaking from experience, this can be overwhelming. At SocialMedia Examiner.com, we don't cover news as it breaks, yet we get at least 5 to 10 people each day asking us to do just that for their companies.

Some Web sites use news stories as the sole source of primary fuel. Others, like SocialMediaExaminer.com, take a slightly different approach.

Rather then racing to be the first to break news, we *do weekly wrap-ups.* Typically, on Saturdays, we summarize what were the biggest news items of the last week. This gives us a bit more time to decide what we should, and should not, report to our reader base.

This also allows us to remain not just a source of informative how-to articles and case studies, but also to be an authority our readers can count on for news that matters. In our case, many of our readers have abandoned our competitors that break 10 to 20 news stories a day, and instead come to us to see what they should focus on.

THE COMPONENTS OF NEWS STORIES

The good news about creating news stories is that they are often much shorter than the typical article. If you're publishing multiple news stories each day, they could be as few as 200 to 400 words. You'll want to include some images in your news stories. If a company has formally announced a product, it will often provide images and written content (and, sometimes, video).

If you become a known source in your industry, you'll often get *news that is embargoed*. This means that a public relations (PR) person from the company will send you advance announcements of what's coming as long as you agree not to write about them until the embargo date has arrived. If you break the embargo, you'll lose the advance notification privilege. The main advantage here is that you can prepare to break a story when it happens.

Many PR people will have articles precrafted for you. This means you can simply edit them and run with them. You can often reach out to businesses and ask to be added to their press notification lists. This will increase the chances you're notified when new news comes out.

Here's an example: An Internet services company named Hurricane Electric had set up a promotional Twitter account indicating how many more days remained until the Web ran out of Internet protocol addresses. It determined that on February 2, 2011, there would be no more of these addresses left.

On January 23, 2011, Mashable.com ran a news story titled, "The Internet Is Running Out of Space . . . Kind of."[1] The opening paragraph of this news story read, "On February 2 around 4 a.m., the Internet will run out of its current version of IP addresses. At least that's what one Internet Service Provider is predicting, based on a rate of about 1 million addresses every four hours." The story went on to quote an expert from *PC World* and explained that the impending deadline really wasn't an issue.

---

[1] Kessler, S. "The Internet Is Running Out of Space . . . Kind of." *Mashable*. January 23, 2011. mashable.com/2011/01/22/the-internet-is-running-out-of-space-kind-of/.

Here are the core elements of a news story:

◆ *The news in a sentence:* The opening line of your news story should summarize the high-level news you want your readers to know.
◆ *A quote:* Ideally, you should seek out a quote, or reference one from a third-party authority that can either add credence or debunk the importance of the news.
◆ *What the news means:* Try to give your readers an early take on what you think about the news. Help them to understand what, if anything, they should do in response to the news.

If you decide to regularly produce news stories, be sure to check out Mashable.com and use its stories as a model for your own. If you decide to do a weekly wrap-up of news stories, search for news on SocialMediaExaminer.com.

Contrarian Stories

When everyone is zigging, do you like to zag? Do you like to question conventional wisdom? If you do, then contrarian stories are for you. *Contrarian stories seek to examine the ugly underbelly of commonly held beliefs and practices.*

Now I'm not suggesting you make it your mission to reveal what's wrong with everything and everyone in your industry. While doing that might gain you some exposure initially, in the long run it will only build a base of readers who share your skepticism. Worse, you might become disrespected in your industry. That said, developing the occasional contrarian article can be a very smart component of your content marketing plan.

For example, I wrote an article called "The Dark Side of Twitter: What Businesses Need to Know," for MarketingProfs.com in February of 2009. That article, released during the peak of the Twitter frenzy, went on to become MarketingProf.com's number-one article of the year. (Appendix E has the article.)

The reason this article was so successful is because I interviewed a number of high-profile marketers who were using Twitter, asking them to share the dark side of their experience with it.

I then crafted an article that also revealed how to overcome those challenges.

Contrarian stories are written using the same steps itemized earlier, in the how-to articles section. The primary difference is that you take a contrarian position on the topic—or at least you appear, at first glance, to do so.

Here are a couple of ideas for topics:

- ◆ Identify what everyone in your industry is talking about. Then decide if it makes sense to develop a contrarian article about those topics.
- ◆ Take a closer look at something that is commonly considered worthless. For example, "Is Newspaper Advertising Really a Useless Effort?"

That covers the six most effective forms of primary fuel. What types would best resonate with your audience?

■ ■ ■

This chapter began by examining the purpose of primary fuel. It then dove deep into the different types of primary fuel you can use to keep your business moving. The six types of primary fuel include: how-to articles, expert interviews, reviews, case studies, news stories, and contrarian stories.

Try experimenting with the different types of fuel. Track the ones that resonate best with your reader base. Be sure to examine the examples in the Appendices A through E.

You should now have a very clear idea of how to create primary fuel.

In the next chapter I introduce you to nuclear fuel—that special content that can propel your rocket ship forward at warp speed.

Creating and Using Nuclear Fuel

Any intelligent fool can make things bigger, more complex, and more violent. It takes a touch of genius—and a lot of courage—to move in the opposite direction.

—Albert Einstein

The primary fuel examined in the prior chapter is essential for the ongoing growth of your business. But sometimes your rocket ship needs a more powerful boost—one that'll have a bigger impact.

If you want to quickly move your business, you'll need to create the most potent type of content—nuclear fuel. When used properly, this advanced propellant will grab the attention of many people and move your rocket ship through space at warp speed.

But nuclear fuel is more difficult to produce, so it's used less frequently and its release must be carefully timed. Most businesses haven't considered this nuclear option; those that do, however, find themselves quickly growing.

In this chapter I will examine the importance of creating nuclear fuel and show you what it can achieve. I'll also provide details on how to create four different types of nuclear fuel.

What Is Nuclear Fuel?

Have you ever experienced a Disney theme park? I remember my first time, as a young kid. My family took a road trip down to Florida to visit my grandparents. Disney World was one of our stops.

I'd dreamed fondly of that day. And when it arrived, I wasn't let down. I entered another world that engaged me at every level. It was a magical experience.

Later, as an adult, I learned what went into creating Disney World: a massive cast, an underground city, and a sophisticated orchestration of technology. These elements together produced the ultimate experience for "children of all ages."

A herculean effort went into the creation of Disney World. In 1963, Walt Disney set out to build the world's most advanced theme park in an obscure location in central Florida.

"For the grand vision to succeed, Disney examined lessons learned from the past and committed to avoiding them in the future," explained Chad Denver Emerson in his book *Project Future*.[1] "In the end, Disney's quest for a Florida project would be built less on pixie dust than on a determined, clever effort to turn an isolated piece of central Florida into one of the world's leading tourist destinations."

Legend has it that Walt Disney lived by this simple mantra: "Dream, Believe, Dare, Do." He was also known for saying, "You can design and create and build the most wonderful place in the world. But it takes people to make the dream a reality."

And Disney executed perfectly, resulting in the world's most popular tourist destination. Even the smallest details of the park were carefully crafted to create an unforgettable experience for guests.

"Every part of the park has its own constant soundtrack (all in the same key and on the same beat, to make for smooth transitions), and there's always a popcorn smell wafting by the entrance," explained a *Washington Post* reporter while recalling a behind-the-scenes tour.[2]

---

[1] Emerson, C.D. *Project Future: The Inside Story Behind the Creation of Disney World* (Ayefour Publishing, 2010).

[2] Hendrix, S. "Behind the Scenes at Disney World," *The Washington Post*, June 18, 2006. www.washingtonpost.com/wp-dyn/content/article/2006/06/16/AR2006061600504 .html.

Why would I open this chapter on creating nuclear fuel with a look at Disney World? What does a childhood adventure park have to do with creating compelling content for businesses?

Walt Disney designed something that had (and continues to have) a deep and lasting effect on people. Disney World's content is composed of entertainment, scripted cast members, elaborate interactive sets, and outstanding music—just to mention a few of its many components.

Disney World is a living and breathing example of nuclear content.

Every word that is spoken, every sound that is heard, and every feature you see there was built and planned with a single purpose: to enable people to connect at a deep level with Disney's message and brand. That connection directly impacts people's desires to invest in anything Disney has to offer, from toys to movies to cruises and beyond.

Don't get me wrong. You don't need to construct a theme park to successfully engage people with nuclear content. But you should *think about the unforgettable response people experience at Disney parks.*

Use Disney's accomplishments to help you understand what can be achieved with nuclear fuel—and the work needed to pull off a Disney-type response.

A Disney experience is built to resonate with all people. Your content likely won't—but that's okay. It's true that written content will rarely elicit the emotional response of a full immersion in a Disney park. The point is to *use Disney World as a metaphor* for your nuclear content. Your goal should be to develop highly valuable content that strongly resonates with the right people—your reader base.

From the moment people first experience your nuclear fuel (i.e., the front gate) to their experience as they tour your content, be sure to wow them.

Nuclear fuel is carefully designed content that has a lasting impact on significant numbers of your ideal reader base—and, sometimes, experts. Nuclear fuel can have a very long shelf life, is highly sharable, and is very valuable to your ideal base.

Nuclear fuel is the successful uncle of primary fuel. What makes it different is the way it's created, packaged, and delivered.

Nuclear fuel is always free and often produced in the form of research reports, white papers, contests, and free online events.

Here's a brief introduction to four types of nuclear fuel:

- ◆ *Reports based on surveys:* This is perhaps the most powerful form of nuclear fuel. When you release free reports based on comprehensive research, you can achieve amazing results. By surveying people in your industry and presenting the results in an easy-to-read report, you can become a thought leader very quickly.
- ◆ *White papers:* These are educational documents designed to help people solve their problems (in much greater detail than an article). They tend to address trends, problems, and solutions. Unlike an article, white papers are usually packaged as PDF files. Unique from other nuclear fuel, white papers can have a very long propulsion period.
- ◆ *Top 10 contests:* People crave recognition. Top 10 contests typically seek nominations and ask people to vote for their favorite company, blog, or book. Contests produce a string of content over a period of time and are interactive. Conducting a well-executed contest can attract power players to your company and lead to amazing exposure.
- ◆ *Micro events:* Webinars, teleclasses, social media events, and live video broadcasts are examples of micro events. These free events are typically one hour in duration and bring an expert of some kind live to your audience. They're more powerful than expert interviews because they're live.

These forms of nuclear fuel are not your only options. But they are the ones I have found to be most effective.

Because nuclear fuel is more difficult to create than primary fuel, you should use it to *supplement* your content marketing, not drive it exclusively. I'll dig deep into how to create each of these forms of nuclear fuel later in the chapter.

Why Does Nuclear Fuel Work?

Nuclear fuel is like a cosmic vacuum cleaner—drawing many people into your amazing content. You should use this type of content when your business needs a boost. For example, if you are just getting under way or are falling behind in your growth, developing some strong nuclear fuel might be wise.

The first two types of nuclear fuel (reports and white papers) are typically long PDF files with rich content. The second two types (contests and events) involve outside experts, have a clear promotional cycle, and are tied to dates.

While these may seem very different at first glance, they accomplish the same purpose: attracting masses of people and delivering highly valuable content.

The reason nuclear fuel is so effective is because it takes gift-giving to an entirely new level.

I discovered the power of nuclear fuel by accident. Back in my days of writing white papers, I conducted a study. My goal was to create a research report and ultimately sell it. And I did just that.

However, I decided to give away my report for free to my newsletter subscribers if they requested it before the end of the year. I ran the promotion for 30 days.

To my amazement, more than 4,000 people downloaded it. But many took it further. They began writing about the report and suggesting to their friends that they check it out. For example, Debbie Weil, author of *The Corporate Blogging Book: Absolutely Everything You Need to Know to Get It Right* (Portfolio Hardcover, 2006), wrote about it on her blog and deemed it one of the best free reports of the year.

I went on to sell the report, but it never really did as well as when I offered it for free. Here's the lesson I learned: When I gave away great free content that my readers would have expected to pay for, they went nuts. *And that exposure was far more valuable than the few dollars I earned selling the actual report.*

Thus, turning your nuclear content into a free gift can lead to priceless exposure.

Here's why each of the following types of nuclear fuel is a gift:

- ◆ *Reports based on surveys:* Most research-type reports are fee-based or are hard to come by. When you choose to give yours away free, you provide a valuable gift to your reader base.

- *White papers:* White papers are typically free. But what makes this content a gift is when it reveals extensive tips and advice on how to solve a problem—without any sales pitches. It becomes a minibook that people will download, print, and regularly reference.
- *Top 10 contests:* There are two types of gifts with this content. First, the winners get the gift of recognition from their peers. Second, your reader base receives a gift by discovering something new among your top 10 winners.
- *Micro events:* Free online events prove to be very valuable gifts for both attendees and presenters. The presenters (often experts) get the gift of exposure. The attendees get the gift of live knowledge and insight from the experts.

Here's how using nuclear fuel will benefit your business:

- Produces a *deep and lasting impact* on your reader base.
- *Exposes your content* to large groups of people, quickly.
- Provides content that has *a long shelf life.*
- Establishes *your business as an authority.*
- *Sets you apart* from competitors.
- Produces *highly sharable* content.
- Grabs the *attention of experts* in your industry.

The benefits of using nuclear fuel are significant. But how does it actually work?

How Does Nuclear Fuel Work?

Where primary fuel gives people a reason to keep coming back to you, *nuclear fuel helps large groups of people discover you.*

If you think of nuclear fuel as a coordinated promotional effort, much like the launch of a product, you'll be able to better grasp its unique power.

Many businesses focus heavily on the release of new products. This might involve joint promotions with partners, special advertising campaigns, and so on.

Nuclear fuel requires a similar effort. However, it's not necessarily tied to a product announcement. Instead, it becomes part of your annual content campaign. Its purpose isn't to sell products but rather to grow your reader base.

Nuclear fuel brings tons of people to you, and your primary fuel keeps them coming back. By releasing a few forms of nuclear content throughout the year, you'll quickly attract a new fan base that will, hopefully, get hooked on your regular content.

Similar to primary fuel, nuclear fuel involves a four-step procedure whereby you create, process, release, and repeat (see Chapter 7). The key distinction of nuclear content is that the creation process can take many weeks. For example, planning for a contest takes a lot of coordination before the "go live" date. Alternatively, writing a report is time-consuming.

The longer creation time means you'll naturally be using less nuclear fuel. The good news is that it can continue to deliver value for months. I've had some nuclear fuel last for five years!

The reason this type of content has such a long shelf life (typically, a year) is because it becomes very popular. That often results in high search engine rankings and people regularly referring the content to others.

Now that you have a clear understanding of why you should use nuclear fuel, let me show you how. For the remainder of this chapter I will explain how to create four types of nuclear fuel: free reports based on surveys, white papers, top 10 contests, and micro events.

Reports Based on Surveys

Releasing original research in the form of a report is one of the most powerful ways to draw attention to your business. *When you create reports based on surveys, you provide insight that is highly valuable to your audience.* When survey data is packaged into a valuable report and released for free, the results can be explosive.

Here's an example of the power of this type of content. In Chapter 4, in the section about fire starters, I shared how I conducted an industry survey and generated a report called the *Social Media Marketing Industry Report* (see Figure 8.1).

We surveyed about 800 marketers, generated a visually appealing 26-page report, and then released it. What happened literally shot our business beyond the stratosphere—overnight.

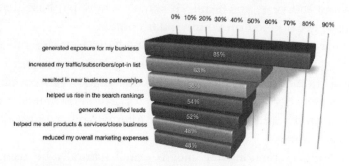

The benefits of social media marketing

The number-one benefit of social media marketing is gaining the all-important eyeball. A significant 85% of all marketers indicated that their social media efforts have generated exposure for their businesses. Improving traffic was the second major benefit, followed by building new partnerships.

More than half of marketers indicated a rise in search engine rankings was a benefit of social media marketing. As search engine rankings improve, so will business exposure, lead generation efforts and a reduction in overall marketing expenses. More than half of marketers found social media generated qualified leads.

Changes since our 2009 study: Every category saw an increase in benefits, except new partnerships remained exactly the same at 56%. In 2009, only 35% of marketers felt social media reduced their overall marketing expenses. That number has jumped to 48%.

Some questions that naturally emerge from the above chart might include, "Can I achieve more benefits by investing more time in social media?", "Are marketers who've been using social media for years gaining even better results?" and "Is there a difference between B2B and B2C?"

The following charts address these questions.

FIGURE 8.1 Here's a sample page from the 2010 *Social Media Marketing Industry Report.*

By 9:00 AM on day one, more than 5,600 people had read the report and 10 bloggers had written about it. After only a week, 22,000 people had read it, more than 100 media outlets had covered it, I'd been on three Internet radio shows, and the report was coming up on the first page of Google for the phrase "social media marketing." Crazy, huh?

I stopped tracking a few weeks later after 40,000 people had read the report. Even a year later the report was still in the top 10 search results on Google.

We went on to release a new report each year with great success. Simply search for *Social Media Marketing Industry Report* to see one of them.

Not only do reports based on surveys provide valuable insight to your reader base, they can also give your business unique market intelligence. With the survey I just referenced, we asked a few extra questions that never made it into the final report. This added intelligence helped us decide how to structure our future offerings.

A second example comes from Ryan Malone of Inside Elder Care, who conducted a number of surveys in the elder care community. For example, he surveyed elder care marketing professionals and produced the *Elder Care Marketing Industry Report*. The report was designed to help establish him as an authority in his space. And he was able to quickly grow his consultancy business. "In less than one year from the date of that survey, I had marketing engagements with three of the top assisted-living providers in the U.S. It was really these tactics that built the foundation for the company," explained Malone.

THE CORE COMPONENTS OF REPORTS BASED ON SURVEYS

Think of these reports like analyst reports. But you don't actually need to be an expert on the topical subject. You gain your knowledge by doing a survey. Your job is to take the resulting data and come up with some unique findings.

Here are the steps involved:

1. *Set up a survey.* Your first task is to come up with a series of questions. For example, you might ask people, "What's the biggest question about social media marketing you most want answered?" Or you could ask people to indicate their agreement with some statements, their future plans, and so on. The point is to come up with the right set of questions whose answers will provide valuable insight to your readers.

I use SurveyMonkey.com to conduct my online surveys. It's very easy to use and allows you to easily run analysis online.

2. *Find people to take the survey.* Using the power of experts and fire starters you can quickly drive the right kinds of people to your survey. I'm not a statistician, but 1,000 people or more is a good goal for coming up with powerful stats. Reaching that number will likely require the help of experts. When I run a survey, I typically leave it open for about two weeks.

3. *Analyze the results.* Survey collection tools like SurveyMonkey .com allow you to easily run most of the analysis you'll need. For example, you can quickly determine how one group answered questions differently than another. In our case, we use the tool to see how age, gender, size of business, and years of experience impact which social media tools people are using.

If you're not superanalytical, or don't have a lot of experience setting up surveys, I strongly suggest you reach out to someone for at least a one-hour consultation. If you call your local university, you'll easily find a graduate student who needs a little side cash. Speak to someone in the psychology, business, or communications graduate division. I'd contact the head of the program and ask for referrals to graduate students who understand SPSS—a statistical analysis program.

4. *Create the report.* Once you have all of your analysis complete, go to work designing a visually appealing final report. I suggest you come up with some nice-looking charts using Excel or Numbers (Mac). One thing to avoid is a dry, boring document. Keep it highly visual. Take a look at the example in Figure 8.1.

The content in your report is very valuable, so you'll want to make it easy to read by including a table of contents and a summary of key findings. I suggest that you carefully study the *Social Media Marketing Industry Report*. You can find it by conducting a simple Google search. Take a close look at the style of writing and the layout.

5. *Release and promote.* Hopefully you offered a free copy of the report as an incentive to the folks who took the survey. If you did, you'll have a nice list of e-mails. You can e-mail those participants and include a direct link to the final report. When

you do that, why not ask them to help spread the word about your new report? Many will, helping make your report popular very quickly. And if you have good relationships with experts and fire starters, ask them to help promote your report, as well.

At SocialMediaExaminer.com we had a little ad designed that directs people to download the free report. It lives in the sidebar on every page of our site. This serves as a great way to generate ongoing power from your report. As new people visit your site, many will discover your report.

Here are some tips for producing effective reports based on surveys:

◆ *Formulate objective survey questions.* Coming up with objective questions is not superintuitive. The poorly formed question will sway your reader, skewing your results. For example, "Is blogging an excellent form of marketing?" would not be objective. The better method way to phrase this question would be: "Please indicate your agreement with the following statement: Blogging helps my marketing," and then ask respondents to strongly agree, agree, disagree, or strongly disagree.

A good free resource is "Designing Surveys That Count," from the Community Research Center at Keene State College, Keene, New Hampshire.[3]

◆ *Ask participants in the survey to help spread the word.* When people are done taking your survey, push them to a special page. On that page ask if they'd be willing to help spread the word so that you can reach your goal of at least 1,000 participants. There, you might also supply some prewritten text they can post on their social networks, along with a link that points people back to your survey.

◆ *Consider calling your survey an "industry" survey.* By including in the title of your survey the word "industry," (e.g., "Time Management Industry Survey"), you'll help people see that they

---

[3] See http://www.keene.edu/crc/forms/designingsurveysthatcount.pdf.

are contributing to something important by taking the time to complete the survey.

◆ *Tell participants what they'll gain by completing the survey.* I would consider promising people who take the survey that they'll get a free copy of the results. That is often a good incentive for them to participate. Just be sure to ask for their e-mail addresses, so you can contact them when your final report is ready.

◆ *Ask experts to reach out to the press on your behalf.* If some of your experts or fire starters have relationships with valuable media outlets, you might want to ask them to share the final report with their sources on your behalf. This allows the message to get through and increases the chances someone else will write about your report.

◆ *Make a video explaining the report results.* Why not record a video showing the results of the survey (see Chapter 7, the reviews section)? In it, you could show people the report and reveal some of its highlights. If you then feature this video on the page with the final report, you could get people excited and increase the chances they'll read your report.

◆ *Make it easy for people to share the final report.* Create some calls to action (see Chapter 5) on the page where your report lives and in the actual report itself. Say something simple like: "If you like this free report, please share it with your peers. Here's how . . . "

Reports based on surveys are extremely powerful forms of nuclear content because they provide brand-new information to your ideal readers and your industry. When you ask the right questions, find some interesting results, and present those findings in an easy-to-read manner, you'll have the best nuclear fuel on the market.

White Papers

I have a soft spot for white papers. In the 2000s, they were the top marketing tool used by businesses selling to other businesses.

White papers were powerful at the time because they signaled the start of a global shift away from reliance on traditional publishers, enabling businesses to release their own content directly to customers.

Today, white papers still have the amazing capability to keep delivering value to your ideal readers. And I'm not talking about those boring technical pieces you may be familiar with. Rather, I'm talking about highly engaging business documents that help people solve problems.

White papers are like articles on steroids. *They are longer educational documents that help people solve specific problems.* They tend to be objective and educational. They are created and distributed by businesses, not in publications. And they sometimes go by different names, like guides, free reports, or ebooks.

Here's a quick example of a white paper I created for FedEx. The title of it was "Speeding the Supply Chain from China." In it I discussed the challenges of shipping products by oceangoing cargo ships and revealed an alternative: overnight air shipments. The FedEx brand wasn't mentioned until the last page.

The white paper, eight pages long, was designed to help electronics manufacturers learn of a newer, faster transit alternative.

These days, most businesses use white papers to generate leads or grow subscriber lists. White papers can have a remarkably long marketing tail. This means that once created, they can deliver value for, literally, years.

Here's another example. In 2003, I wrote a white paper called "How to Write a White Paper: A White Paper on White Papers" (see Figure 8.2).

My objective was to create an educational piece that revealed some of my trade secrets in the paper. These were my best tips, and I just gave them away. This was a novel idea at the time because other businesses were focusing on their speeds, feeds, products, and services—not educating.

My hope was that some readers would see that I was an expert and ultimately hire me to help them create their own white papers.

Here's what ended up happening: That paper helped me land big names like Microsoft, FedEx, Dow Jones, and HP as clients. It also

STELZNER CONSULTING

How to Write a White Paper
A White Paper on White Papers

By Michael A. Stelzner

About the Author: Michael Stelzner is the author of *Writing White Papers: How to Capture Readers and Keep Them Engaged*, the executive editor of the 20,000-reader *WhitePaperSource™ Newsletter* and has written more than 130 papers for major corporations such as Microsoft, FedEx, Motorola, Dow Jones, LinkedIn, HP, Monster, and SAP.

So you've decided you need a white paper. What exactly should the objectives be? Will the paper be well-received? How long should it be? Who will write it? These and many other questions are common concerns that should be addressed from the start. The good news is you are not alone! Since its first edition, more than 85,000 people have read this paper. It is my hope that it leads you in the right direction.

This paper's objective is to guide you in the process of developing effective white papers and persuasive business documents.

What Is a White Paper?

The term *white paper* is an offshoot of the term *white book*, which is an official publication of a national government. A famous white paper example is the *Winston Churchill White Paper of 1922*, which addressed political conflict in Palestine.

A white paper usually argues a specific position or solution to a business problem

A white paper typically argues a specific position or solution to a problem. Although white papers take their roots in governmental policy, they have become a common tool used to introduce technology innovations and products. A typical search engine query on "white paper" will return millions of results, with many focused on technology-related issues.

White papers are powerful marketing tools used to help key decision-makers and influencers justify implementing solutions. For some examples of white papers used in the technology marketplace, see http://www.stelzner.com/copy-whitepapers.html.

FIGURE 8.2 This is the front page of a white paper I wrote that transformed my business.

became required reading at respected universities like Johns Hopkins and MIT.

That single paper also led to a bestselling book (*Writing White Papers* was in its fourth printing when I wrote this book), and my industry peers referring to me as the "king of white papers."

Another amazing outcome was that I generated an enormous number of leads. The first year I got 4,260 leads; the second brought in an additional 10,099; the third year there were 13,255 more; the fourth year, another 14,285; the fifth year, 13,055 more; the sixth year added 15,539; and the seventh year brought in an additional 15,074 leads. I stopped counting after 85,000.

Yes, the same paper delivered leads for more than seven years! And these weren't poor-quality leads. A random sampling from one day included companies like Computer Associates, Booze Allen Hamilton, the U.S. Department of Veteran Affairs, *The Denver Post*, and Blue Cross/Blue Shield.

White papers are a powerful form of nuclear content. What goes into producing one?

THE CORE COMPONENTS OF WHITE PAPERS

High-quality white papers focus on problems and provide solutions. The goal is to build affinity with your readers by focusing on their problems. If they can relate to your writing, they'll be eager to keep reading so they can discover how to solve their problems.

There are five primary sections of educational white papers: trends, problems, solutions, history, and benefits.

Trends   After the opening paragraphs of your white paper, you'll want to start talking about trends. Trends explain where the world is headed. They add credibility and draw people deeper into your document. When you write about trends, ideally you should refer to known third-party sources.

For example, "By 2015, 81 percent of all businesses will be using social media to engage with customers and prospects," said Michael Stelzner, founder of SocialMediaExaminer.com. I just made that up for this example, but you get the idea.

If your white paper were an educational piece on how businesses could benefit from social media, having similar trend statements would strengthen your work.

Problems   By talking about problems, for starters, you'll be validating concerns your readers have. In addition, you might introduce issues they've never considered before. All along the way, you're going to be building affinity. Problems have to be clearly identified and relevant to your ideal readers.

For example, "Many businesses struggle to track the return on investment for social media efforts. They know there are benefits, but they simply can't quantify them to upper management."

When you write about problems, state them clearly. Then back them up with supporting data. Talk about what happens when people don't actually deal with those problems.

Ideally, you'll pick a few problems to focus on in this section of your white paper.

History   History is really meaningful because people find it interesting. Including it also helps to establish your expertise. When you discuss history, try focusing on how problems have been solved in the past, or how things have evolved.

Here's an example: "The earliest social media tools were rudimentary bulletin boards systems used in the 1980s. They allowed people to post messages and reply via dial-up models."

Keep the history section short, and use it as a bridge to your suggested solution(s).

The Solution   Here is where you reveal how to solve the problems identified earlier in your paper. And when you introduce your solutions without mentioning a company or product, you increase the chances your readers will stick with the paper—making it educational rather than sales-focused.

Here's an example: "New social media tracking tools make it easy for businesses to directly connect social media activities to sales." If I were writing this piece in full, I'd go on to explain what these tools are and how they work.

Benefits   Benefits address the innate desire of every human being to know "What's in it for me?" When you talk about benefits, make sure you use action verbs like "improves," "simplifies," and "reduces."

Why Most Writing Is Never Read

Have you ever wondered, "Who reads this stuff?" Most of what I read bores me to death. Here are a few thoughts on why most content is of such poor quality:

Immediate sale: Bad writing gives me no reason to stay engaged. Rather than easing into a topic, it simply assumes the reader is "up to speed" on the subject at hand (e.g., "Get the Remco hair remover now by calling 1-800-We-Need-Your-Money").

Long-winded: Remember those boring textbooks that had paragraphs that spanned multiple pages? The brain is wired for breaks; that's why we have a Return key on our keyboards. Try having a conversation with someone who can't get to the point and you'll understand why long paragraphs are boring.

No logical flow: This may seem simple, but a story has a beginning, middle, and an end. Too often, poor writing is missing one or more of these basic elements. If you're selling video software, begin with the challenges faced by video folks, talk about how to solve the problem (the middle), and then tell readers where to buy the product (the end).

Here are important tips for creating white papers:

◆ *Spend some effort on the first page.* Be sure to create a title and opening paragraph that really grab people. Because white papers are much longer than articles, work hard to give readers a reason to want to spend the time reading your paper. This means craft your opening page like a movie trailer: Reveal a few enticing points that encourage people to keep reading.
◆ *Divulge your best ideas.* Make sure you don't hold anything back in your white paper. If you've got a no-fail technique for solving a problem, lay it out in the paper. You'll build enormous

goodwill with your readers and increase the likelihood they'll share your paper with others.

◆ *Resist the urge to sell something.* Traditionally, white papers are ideal for selling. However, to strengthen your content marketing efforts, limit any mention of your products or services to the last page. Your white paper should be educational. If it smells like a sales piece, your readers will toss it in the trash.

Want to know more? For an in-depth understanding of how to create effective white papers, check out my last book, *Writing White Papers: How to Capture Readers and Keep Them Engaged* (go to WritingWhitePapers.com/book).

Should You Give Away Your Secrets?

Does it make sense to share the very secrets that make you successful? The simple answer is *yes*.

You see, no matter how much you reveal in your white paper, it still won't come even close to what you bring to the table. And no one can do it like you can.

By sharing your secrets with your readers, you will convey your expertise to them and, oftentimes, compel them to contact you to learn more.

Here's a case in point: My previous book contains hundreds of pages on how to craft white papers, yet I was regularly contacted by businesses that wanted to hire me. Get the picture?

The key take-home message is this: You must provide very valuable information to your ideal readers to prove to them that you are indeed an expert. The typical response will be, "If he shared all this great knowledge, how much more will I gain by working with his company?"

Top 10 Contests
And now for something completely different.

Contests are a unique form of nuclear fuel because they're interactive and thus engage your reader base in a way more passive forms of fuel cannot.

Top 10 contests invite your readers to nominate their favorite people, products, blogs, or businesses. Typically, a panel of experts determines the ultimate winners. Think one part People's Choice Awards and one part Oscars.

Winners of top 10 contests are not gaining anything they can wrap their hands around. Instead, they're gaining something that's intangible but often more important: their names in lights, so to speak. They receive a badge of honor they can display on their Web site, announcing they've won something prestigious, hence of great value. *Nearly everyone loves to see their names in lights.*

You might be wondering why in the world you should consider a contest as part of your content strategy. Here are the benefits of contests:

- ◆ *Excites your readers.* Contests allow your readers to get involved and become engaged. Often, a good contest can generate a high level of excitement.
- ◆ *Drives traffic.* Contests are also an effective way to increase the traffic to your Web site. People will naturally drive others to your site during the promotional and announcement phases of a contest.
- ◆ *Attracts experts.* You can bring experts to the table as judges, giving them amazing exposure. Often, the winners of top 10 contests are the types of people you'd want to develop relationships with.
- ◆ *Inspires goodwill.* When you host a contest, you're seen as an arbitrator of goodwill to your industry. You're naturally excluded from the running.

The other-focused nature of this type of contest is regarded as admirable by your peers.

THE CORE COMPONENTS OF TOP 10 CONTESTS

To best demonstrate what goes into top 10 contests, I'm going to share a case study.

In December of 2009, SocialMediaExaminer.com launched the Top 10 Social Media Blogs contest, designed to reveal the best blogs in the industry. We were about two months old at the start of the contest.

Our objective was to attract the attention of important industry players, increase exposure of our site, and grow our subscriber base. Our hope was that by driving people to the contest, they'd learn about us, discover our educational content, and want to sign up for our free daily e-mail blasts.

The contest was also meant to be a *recruitment mechanism*. My hope was that experts would see the power of our site and be willing to speak at our events. And that's exactly what ended up happening.

We ran the promotion for about 45 days. *We started with a blog post asking people to nominate their favorite social media blogs.*

In order for a blog to win, it needed at least two nominations. This was important because it forced bloggers who wanted to win to seek the support of others (naturally drawing people to our promotion). The winners gained prestige and an attractive badge they could place on their blog (see Figure 8.3).

FIGURE 8.3 The badge awarded to winners of our Top 10 Social Media Blogs contest.

We also recruited three known industry experts to be judges. This was important because we were pretty much unknown in the industry at the time.

Here's a quick preview of the results. The contest:

- Appeared on the first page of Google for "top 10 blogs" searches.
- Appeared on the first page of Delicious.
- Led to more than 7,600 people visiting the page listing the winners.

Here were the phases of the contest:

Phase 1: Nominations from Fans   First, people came to our blog and nominated someone by leaving a comment on the blog. Two nominations were required for a nominee to be considered.

This produced a crazy viral effect because bloggers started noticing that people were nominating them. They wanted to win this contest, so people started tweeting about it to their fan bases, and going on Facebook and asking their friends, "Please, if you like our blog, would you nominate us? We want to win this contest."

Phase 2: Determining the Finalists   The second phase involved removing every site that wasn't a social media blog and identifying only those people who had two or more nominations. Those names became the finalists.

We published an article congratulating the finalists (listing them in alphabetical order). In the post we also gave a shoutout to the judges, thanking them for their involvement (and linking back to their sites).

This also became a second opportunity, after the nominations, for us to generate more buzz. Now the finalists could get excited and say, "Thank you to all my fans for their nominations," which lots of them did. Many also wrote articles on their blogs expressing their gratitude to be among the finalists.

Phase 3: Choosing the Winners   The final phase of the contest involved selecting the winners. The judges, naturally, played a big part in this phase.

We were very strategic from the beginning to choose high-profile judges. We asked Scott Monty, head of social media for Ford Motor Company. We also recruited Ann Handley, chief content officer from MarketingProfs.com. Our third pick was David Meerman Scott, author of the bestselling book *New Rules of Marketing & PR.*

I'll give you a little insight into how we recruited this group. I sent private Twitter messages to all three of them at the same time, but altering each a little. To Scott Monty, I wrote, "Scott, would you be willing to be on a panel to judge a social media contest with David Meerman Scott and Ann Handley?" I wrote the exact same thing to Ann: "Ann, would you be willing to join Scott Monty and David Meerman Scott?"

Almost immediately all three responded, "Yes, I'd be happy to." I never actually said to any one of them that the other two were already onboard. But I knew they all knew each other—and me to some extent—so I was able to get them all.

How We Selected the Winners   We came up with a formula to determine the top 10 winners. We placed the most weight on the assessment of the judges. We simply asked them to come up with a score based on the quality of the blogs they reviewed. That was the full extent of the judges' involvement.

We then averaged the scores together, coming up with a number between 1 and 55. Thus, the judges' votes totaled 55 percent. The remaining 45 percent was based on a quantitative assessment of a number of factors. For example, we looked at how often the nominees posted on their blog. Obviously, if they were infrequent, they didn't get as high a score.

We also added up the number of nominations they received, along with the number of comments on their blog. Finally, we examined public blog rankings. We relied on Technorati's rankings to make up a small component of the final score.

We combined all these factors to calculate the final scores. The top 10 winners were the blogs with the highest overall scores.

How We Announced the Winners   We created a third blog post listing the winners. We also displayed the badge of distinction (see the badge shown in Figure 8.3). We encouraged the winners to post it on their

Web sites as long as they agreed to link back to the page listing the winners.

The Winners' Responses   The responses from the winners were pretty phenomenal. One of them, Jason Falls, posted this comment, "This is an honor for two reasons. We were nominated by readers of [Social Media] Examiner—which has quickly become a great resource for smart people—and the three judges are people I truly admire."

Jay Baer's response was: "Delighted and honored to be in such company . . . " and he went on to thank all the people who helped him get started.

It was thrilling to see high-profile people coming to the page and commenting on the results. Many of them shared the honor with their audiences, driving even more traffic to our site.

How the Winners Used the Award   The winners did some amazing things with the award. For example, Jason Falls referenced that he was the winner of the Social Media Examiner Top 10 Social Media Blogs for 2010 in the first sentence of his biography, with a link directly to our site.

A number of the winners put the award on their Web sites, and it showed up on every page of their blog. The badge displayed our brand and linked directly to our Web site.

The Marketing Results   First, we received an enormous amount of exposure for our brand-new Web site—especially among major industry players. Almost immediately, a lot of these gurus began referring to our Web site as a top site. Shortly thereafter, we started winning all sorts of awards as a high-quality resource. Broader recognition became very important for us.

We still get a lot of traffic to this day to the winner's page. It also helped our search engine optimization rankings because many people (beyond the winners) took the findings from our contest and created their own blog posts and linked right back to our page.

Top 10 contests don't need to be focused only on blogs. You could just as easily focus on top 10 books, top 10 tools, top 10 professionals in your industry, and so on. Just follow the model detailed here and watch what happens.

Tips for Conducting Top 10 Contests

Here are some pointers to help your contest go smoothly:

◆ *Choose reputable judges.* Recruit judges who are known in your industry, and then make it easy for them to participate. Let them know what's in it for them. Share with the judges how you'll promote them. For example, you could promise they'll be mentioned and linked to at all stages of the promotion.

◆ *Make sure to give your readers a voice.* Don't rely fully on the judges for your final score. Enable your readers to play a part by counting the numbers of nominations from them. I suggest you do more than just ask for a nomination; ask readers also to explain why they're making their nominations. For example, "Nominate your favorite blogger, and be sure to tell us why you think he or she should win." This also gets nominees excited when they read what others think about them.

◆ *Hire a designer.* Invest in creating a really cool badge of distinction, one that people would be proud to put up on their sites. Two outstanding illustrators are Court Patton (pattonbros .com) and Gregory Grigoriou (vanpaul.com).

◆ *Actively seek nominations.* Don't just announce, "Here are the top 10 winners." Instead, ask people to nominate the winners. That allows you to establish all the different phases. Remember, each one is a PR opportunity for your Web site.

Top 10 contests are a unique and powerful form of nuclear content because they engage your reader base and are very valuable to experts. Be sure to study the way SocialMediaExaminer.com uses this form of nuclear fuel and apply what you discover to your own contests.

Micro Events

Strategic online events can engage your audience and provide you a powerful way to connect with experts. *Micro events are free live activities that take place online and last for about an hour.* Webinars, social media events, Internet radio shows, teleclasses, and live video broadcasts are all examples of micro events. The reason I'm using the word "micro" is because these types of events are short in duration and are far less complicated than multisession or multiday seminars.

These free events typically bring an expert live to your audience, and are more powerful than expert interviews because they're in real time. Live events have a special ability to attract lots of people—and experts.

Here's an example of a micro event. A few times a month, SocialMediaExaminer.com conducts Facebook Friday expert sessions. We invite a book author or well-known social media expert to answer questions on our Facebook wall for an hour.

We promote the event and the expert guest for a few days before it takes place. On the day and hour of the event, our readers flock to our Facebook wall and ask the expert questions (see Figure 8.4). It's a fun and engaging time when the expert shares his or her particular scope of knowledge. And sometimes our Facebook fans chime in with their advice, as well.

By the end of the hour the expert is gratified to have interacted with so many people, and your fans love getting their questions answered by experts.

Whether your micro event is a webinar, live video broadcast, an Internet radio show, or some other activity, the *benefits of micro events are significant for your business*:

◆ *Connects your fans to your business.* Micro events transform people from passive lurkers to active participants. When that happens, the chances they'll evangelize your brand greatly improve.

◆ *Allows you to build stronger relationships with experts.* By giving experts a platform from which to interact with your audience, you'll forge stronger bonds with experts. Forming those bonds could be an important step toward nurturing an expert to become a fire starter.

◆ *Provides highly valuable content to your base.* The information that experts share is very valuable to visitors to your site. And having the opportunity to ask direct questions of experts meets a desire of many people.

Social Media Examiner Angie Swartz asks: I'd love to hear Jeff talk about how to get fans to chat more directly on the page. Fans seem to like to email or send FB messages privately more than to talk openly on our Square Martini page. Ideas?
2,403 Impressions · 0.33% Feedback

September 3 at 10:09am · Comment · Like · Promote

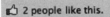 2 people like this.

 Jonathan E. Seely Ask questions. Questions lead to discussion and side conversations.
September 3 at 10:12am · Like · Delete

 Jeff Widman By chat, I assume you mean "write on the wall"?? (There are some custom applications that DO allow real-time chatting... like if you have your VP of product chat directly with your Facebook fans and answer their questions)
September 3 at 10:15am · Like · Delete

 Jeff Widman Assuming you mean write on the wall, I actually think we need to back up a bit. (heads up--key point!)

95% of people interact with fan pages via the newsfeed, NOT by going to the fan page and writing on the wall. So if you're trying to force...
See More
September 3 at 10:18am · Like · 👍 1 person · Delete

 Jeff Widman So in actuality, it's MUCH, MUCH better to focus on "How do I get fans to interact with my status updates in their newsfeed??" rather than "How do I get fans to write on my wall?"
September 3 at 10:19am · Like · Delete

 Jan McCorkle @Jeff questions are good. are there other tips to engage fans and encourage writing on the wall
September 3 at 10:20am · Like · Delete

 Jeff Widman @Jan--totally. There's a number of other tips. We recently were able to help a client become the fastest growing fan page in all of Facebook over a 3 week period, using only newsfeed optimization.
September 3 at 11:25am · Like · 👍 2 people · Delete

FIGURE 8.4 Here's an example of Facebook expert Jeff Widman answering questions during one of SocialMediaExaminer.com's Facebook Friday events.

Now that you're beginning to see the power of micro events, the next logical question is, "What's involved in presenting them?"

THE CORE COMPONENTS OF MICRO EVENTS

Regardless of the platform, there are a number of core elements that go into the planning and production of any micro event. Your job will be to master the basics and then alter them slightly depending on whether you're hosting a webinar, a Facebook event, or some other activity.

There are four primary steps involved in producing a micro event.

Recruit an Expert   Ideally, find someone who is passionate about his or her area of expertise and communicates well. Act like you're a movie producer casting a lead actor. Remember, the expert will be in front of your audience, so you'll want someone who can deliver the goods.

If there's a speaking role, I suggest you search on YouTube to see if the expert has spoken before. Check to see if he or she has a stage presence, and speaks well. This is very important. Not all big names are comfortable in front of audiences. You want someone with deep knowledge and great communication skills.

Once you find the right expert to recruit, be sure to explain the benefits of participating to him or her. Simply put yourself in the shoes of the expert and ask, "What's in it for them?" Often, experts are seeking to promote a book, mention a new project, or are hoping to gain more exposure. (See the section on working with outside experts in Chapter 4 for more ideas on how to recruit experts.)

Once you have the interest of an expert, describe how the event will work and what to expect. Many people forget this critical step. The more comfortable your expert feels about what will take place, the better he or she will be able to deliver great content—and commit to you.

Promote the Event   One strong reason experts will participate in your events is because of the promotional opportunity. Therefore, you'll want to make sure the name of the expert and his or her credentials are displayed prominently in all of your event promotions.

Use multiple channels to get the word out about your event. For example, SocialMediaExaminer.com uses e-mail, Facebook, and Twitter to drive people to our micro events.

A word of caution is in order here: Never expect experts to promote your micro event for you. Their valuable time is their gift to you. When you respect that by not asking for anything in return, they will respect you in turn. Many experts will promote your event without your asking, but don't count on it and don't ask for it.

Prepare Questions in Advance Because most micro events are simply live interviews of experts, it's important to prepare your questions in advance. And if you'll mostly be relying on your reader base to pose questions, consider soliciting your readers in advance for theirs. This will help you slide through slow periods where no one seems to have anything to say. It will also come in handy if the expert is quickly moving through your prepared questions.

You might also consider sharing the extra questions in advance with your expert. I've found this helps the person plan for what may be coming.

Direct the Live Event Explain to people how to participate in the event, and introduce the expert to them, as there's a pretty good chance some people in your audience won't be familiar with the person. And when you introduce the expert, be sure to mention his or her accomplishments.

As you begin taking questions, it's a good idea to regularly remind listeners how to participate. You might say something as simple as, "As a reminder, please call the number on your screen to ask your question of our expert."

At the conclusion of your event, thank your expert, and be sure to allow him or her to plug his or her latest project, book, or Web site.

Here are more tips to enhance your micro event:

- *Check the presenter's audio.* If your expert will be speaking, it's a good idea to test his or her audio *prior* to the event going live. Ask experts if there might be any dogs, children, or other noises where they're speaking from that could detract from the sound quality. Also request that your experts turn off any mobile devices, and mute their computers, in advance. You also might need to ask your expert to speak up or work on his or her projection.
- *Be prepared for technical challenges.* With micro events, it's not a question of *if* you'll experience a technical hiccup, it's a question of *when*. So put backup plans in place for technology that is most likely to fail. For audio, ask the presenter to have a mobile phone handy, in case something goes wrong. For a webinar, you may need to plan for a voice-only discussion, if

the connection dies or the computer crashes. Leverage the old Boy Scout motto: Be prepared.

♦ *Prepare for nonstop talkers.* If you'll be taking live callers during your micro event, you may get someone who wants to talk endlessly. Your expert might even be one of this type. You'll want to have an action plan for dealing with this dilemma. I suggest you provide a way for people to take the discussion off-line if it's going on too long. You could suggest, for example, "Why don't you put that up on our Facebook page?" or "E-mail me after the call and we can go into more detail. Thanks for the question."

♦ *Offer a thank-you gift to the expert.* You may want to consider giving a gift to the expert as your way of saying thanks. It could be something as small as a Starbucks gift card or even a handwritten thank-you note. Such small tokens of appreciation go a long way with experts.

Micro events can be a lot of fun and are far less complicated than other forms of nuclear fuel. If you've never done one before, experiment with one and see how it works for your business.

■ ■ ■

I began this chapter by examining the purpose of nuclear fuel. I then dove deep into four different types of fuel you can use to give your business quick boosts. The four types of nuclear fuel include reports based on research, white papers, top 10 contests, and micro events.

Nuclear fuel does take more effort to produce than primary fuel; however, this type of content can have a longer-lasting impact on your readers, as well as draw experts to your business.

Start paying attention to how other businesses use nuclear fuel. Then, when you're ready, apply what you've learned and prepare for rapid growth.

In Chapter 9, the last chapter, I focus on marketing and how you can use it to grow your business.

How to Employ Marketing

To go places and do things that have never been done before—that's what living is all about.

—Michael Collins, Apollo 11 astronaut

When you can hold back the marketing messages from your content, it will take your business to unimaginable places. But the idea of restraining marketing messages is a difficult pill for most people to swallow. It's the opposite of what many marketers believe to be right and true.

One of my favorite movies of all times is *Braveheart,* in which Mel Gibson plays the Scottish warrior William Wallace. There's a scene in the movie where Wallace's men are standing ready for battle. Galloping toward his company is a massive opposing force, armed with lances. Wallace screams out, repeatedly, "Hold. Hold. Hold. Hold." Every bone in his men's bodies wants to leap forward into battle. But Wallace restrains them.

Then, just as the opposing army gets within a few yards of his men, Wallace yells, "Now!" His men quickly arch long spikes—a horse's height above the ground—effectively erecting a wall of death that annihilates their opposition. They win the battle by exercising restraint.

In a similar way, you can achieve your marketing objectives if you know how to exercise marketing restraint.

In this, the final chapter of *Launch*, I will show you the best ways to employ marketing messages when content is the fuel of your business. It will also reveal a proven method for selling your products and services without offending your readers.

What Does "Caging Marketing Messages" Mean?

Recall that the elevation principle equation is: Great Content plus Other People minus Marketing Messages.

What does the "minus marketing messages" part really mean?

Too often, businesses treat people like fish. We've been taught wrong. The old mantra says that if you simply drop the right message on the heads of the right people, they'll bite. That lure has lost its luster. It no longer works.

In an age where your future customers have endless choices and increasing control over media, it's time for us to rethink the way we market.

In the old world, all you had to do was "pay to play." The goal was to place the right ads in the few places where people "hung out." That model is rapidly becoming ineffective in today's world. Witness the demise of print publications and newspapers as proof that consumers have moved on. They no longer have limited media consumption choices.

If you continue to make paid placements the center of your marketing strategy, you'll always be reliant on others, and may quickly run out of money.

In the new world, *consumers go where they find the best value.* When your business becomes a publisher of great content, it transforms into a magnetic force that attracts many people. This causes your rocket ship to quickly accelerate. As this happens, you'll gain opportunities to employ new marketing tactics. Rather than your business chasing people, they'll be chasing you.

Here are some reasons why most forms of advertising will let you down. *People are very good at ignoring marketing messages.* With the exception of the Super Bowl, can you think of another situation where you actually enjoy watching commercials? If you're like me, commercials are an excuse to leave the room. The same is true of all other mediums.

On Web sites, do you enjoy reading articles that flow around large animated ads? What about those sites where banner ads take up every square inch of virtual real estate? Does anyone really look at them?

If you think about it, most ads are designed to distract people from your content, not draw them in. Advertisers hope to "steal" people from the very places where they advertise. And too many publishers are more than willing to subject their readers to endless ads and promotions, hoping to make a few dollars.

Now, if you own your own platform (perhaps a blog), do you really want to send people away? What about your own products and services? Should you heavily advertise them in place of other ads? Will your readers ignore them as well?

If you want to rapidly grow your reader base, you'll want to "cage your marketing messages." By that I mean you should greatly limit, or omit entirely, obvious advertisements from your site and your content. I also mean that you should refrain from referencing your services in most of your content.

When you remove all marketing messages, your content becomes a true gift to consumers. When you display blatant or excessive marketing messages, people will see your content for what it is: bait to get them to "bite," to purchase something.

But is there a middle ground?

How to Employ Marketing Messages

Naturally the question arises, "When *can* I market?" or "How *should* I market?" Clearly, you're producing content to build a following. And when you have loyal fans, this opens up the opportunity for you to market and sell your products and services.

Here's the good news: There are plenty of ways to market with content. They're just not obvious at first glance. What follows are some proven ideas that I hope will show you alternative ways to market with content.

MARKETING FOR LEADS

Here's a new way to think about your marketing. *Create marketing messages that drive people to your content, not your products and services.*

Change your focus. When you do this, you can actively market your content with the intent of generating leads. Rather than making the sale a goal of your advertising, your objective becomes getting people to subscribe to some of your nuclear content.

This becomes a friction-free first step. If you make it easy for people to take that step, they'll move closer to becoming customers. Something free can lead to future fees.

Here's a simple analogy. Have you ever wandered by an ice cream shop and the server behind the counter offered, "Would you like to sample a flavor?" You likely tried a few and then ordered a cone. In a similar, yet prolonged way, properly marketed content can move people into a process that results in many eventual sales. That content is your ice cream sample.

Here's how it works. You *take some of your nuclear content—like webinars, white papers, or reports—and ask people to register for free access to them.* This becomes an entry point for future customers and a way to capture prospects' contact details.

In his book *Lead Generation for the Complex Sale*, Brian Carroll introduced the concept of lead nurturing. He explained that lead nurturing "keeps the conversation going over time, building solid relationships and allowing the creation of interest in products and/or services while bringing leads to a sales-ready status when the buying opportunity presents itself."[1]

The process of nurturing leads starts with people registering for special content. Over time, you'll feed those people more relevant content with the hope that someday some of them will be ready to purchase.

Here's an example. I used the method just described to grow my white paper writing business. I started with a free one called, "How to Write a White Paper." When all of my competitors were advertising,

---

[1] Carroll, B.R. *Lead Generation for the Complex Sale: Boost the Quality and Quantity of Leads to Increase Your ROI* (New York: McGraw-Hill, 2006).

"Hire a white paper writer," I was advertising, "What Is a White Paper? Free How-to Guide."

Simply put, I met people where their need was with my ads. Rather than trying to sell them, I gave them something free and valuable—a how-to piece of nuclear content.

I then sent a subset of people who registered for my paper monthly e-mails with valuable articles on writing and marketing white papers. I knew not everyone was ready for my type of service. But when they were, I wanted to be the first person they contacted. I used my e-mails as a way to remain top-of-mind with prospects.

Most of the times I sent those articles, people e-mailed me back asking for quotes. When prospects contacted me, most were ready to purchase. I was able to generate $30,000 a month in writing contracts using this system.

When you promote your free content, you'll generate the highest possible response rate to your advertising. And those ads can live on your site or be placed elsewhere online. The reason this works is because there's no perceived advertising bias with these types of ads.

If you advertise a free report or a free webinar, you'll get a large response, regardless of the medium. Why? *People regard this form of advertising as content, not a sales pitch.*

The keyword to use in your ads is "free." When people know you're not actively selling something, they'll be more likely to click on your ads. Research by social scientist Dan Zarrella affirms that the word "free" can help increase the chances people will register for content.[2]

Once people click, you'll send them to a page introducing your nuclear content. Then simply ask them to complete a form to gain free access to your content. Each person who fills out the form should be put on a special list and be considered a possible lead.

Here's another example. HubSpot effectively uses content to generate leads. It often gets many thousands of new leads each time it hosts a webinar (see Figure 9.1). The webinar itself contains

---

[2] Zarrella, D. "Data: Free Stuff and Contests Work for Lead Generation," *HubSpot's Inbound Marketing Blog*, October 12, 2010.

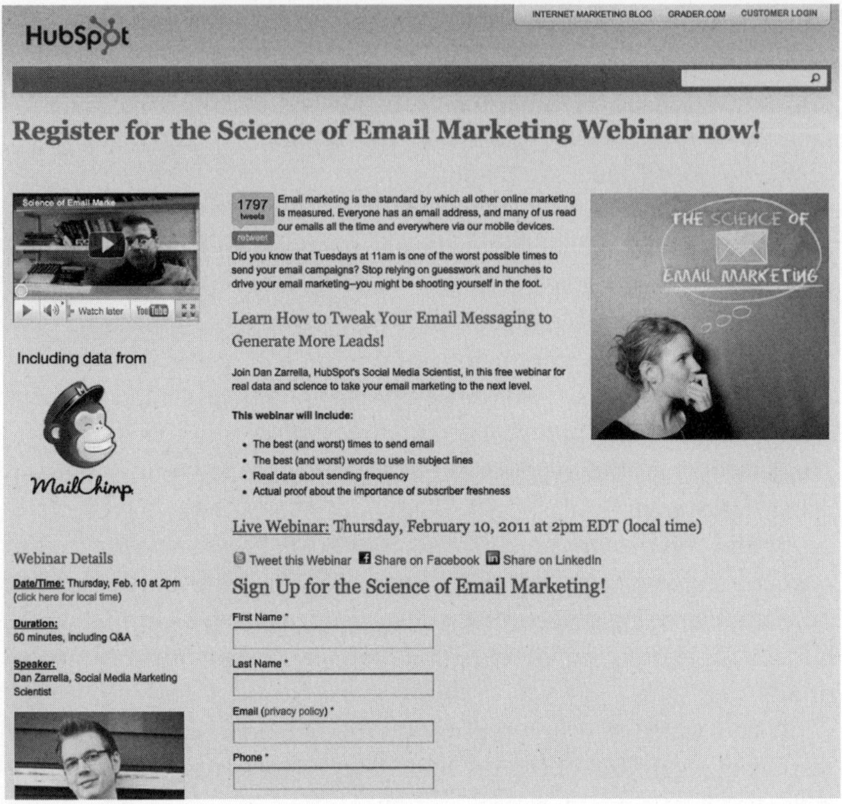

FIGURE 9.1 Here's an example of how HubSpot uses webinars to capture leads.

Source: Reproduced by permission from HubSpot © February 10, 2011.

no pitch for HubSpot's services. However, a HubSpot sales team follows up with leads after the webinar.

This is a very effective model for HubSpot because the company is delivering high value content with zero marketing messages. And attendees feel little or no advertising bias because leads are nurtured after the great content has been delivered.

Note, too, that HubSpot salespeople don't immediately go for the sale. Instead, they send more free content to further qualify prospects, greatly increasing their conversion rates.

Here's another example. Hoover's, Inc., experimented with banner ads focused on free content. The company found that its most effective ad read, simply: "Get a free white paper on how to prep for cold calls." Consequently, this ad accounted for more than one-third of its total ad clicks and total leads across all of its marketing campaigns.[3]

Using ads to drive people to your nuclear content is an effective way to begin employing marketing messages and generating leads. Not all of your nuclear fuel should be used for lead generation, however, but if your ultimate goal is to generate prospects for your business, there's no better way to do it than with the methods I just outlined.

There are other ways you can use marketing messages. But first you need a way to capture and retain your reader base.

PROMOTING YOUR SUBSCRIPTIONS AND NETWORKS

Primary and nuclear fuel will draw many people to your content. If you want a powerful opportunity to market to potential customers, you'll need to *encourage people to subscribe to your content updates or join your social media communities*. These become secondary communication channels that can lead to significant marketing opportunities.

When you publish great content, some of your readers will want to know when you plan to release more. Coming up with systems to move those people to your e-mail lists, your Facebook pages, or other social networks is essential. The goal is to make it easy for people to receive updates from your business.

This is the key to opening marketing doors in the future. For example, if people opt in to receive e-mail updates from you, they've given you direct access to their inboxes—a powerful privilege that shouldn't be taken lightly.

When people join your Facebook page and engage, they're giving you access to their newsfeeds. These types of opportunities are golden, when used properly. *When people give you permission to send them your content, this opens up new marketing channels*—ones that you can market through.

---

[3] Gault, K. "Case Study: How Hoover's Is Using White Papers to Nurture Leads," *WhitePaperSource Newsletter*, July, 2010. www.whitepapersource.com/case-studies/casestudy-hoovers/.

E-mail is the most important channel for you to cultivate. Unlike social networks, when you grow a list of e-mail subscribers, it's *your* list. You can take it from one e-mail provider to the next. You can communicate to your list as often as you want. You have full control, and e-mail is a very powerful marketing channel.

You should *come up with a system that encourages people to sign up for e-mail notifications.* Here's how we do it at SocialMedia Examiner.com. We use a pop-up box that shows up only for first-time visitors to the site (see Figure 9.2). We invite these newcomers to join our free e-mail newsletter, explaining that they'll be notified by e-mail when we release new content. *We incentivize people to subscribe by offering a free and exclusive social media video tutorial.*

This method of capturing e-mails accounts for nearly 74 percent of all of our subscribers. We also embed a small form in the sidebar of

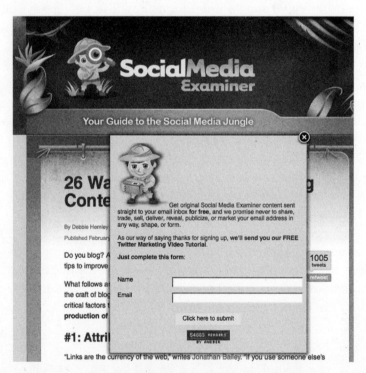

FIGURE 9.2 SocialMediaExaminer.com uses a pop-up box to incentivize first-time visitors to subscribe to a newsletter.

our site that makes a similar offer. In addition, we post the words "Free Subscription" in a prime location on the top navigation bar.

Through these steps we've made transforming people from page viewers to e-mail subscribers a top priority on our site. And it has worked very well. Within the first 12 months of the site's launch, we had 40,000 double-opted-in e-mail subscribers.

Once people have subscribed, we use an automated system that e-mails them each morning we have a new post (see Figure 9.3). The e-mail contains a short summary of the day's article, with a link to the site. It also contains occasional promotions for our nuclear content. We use Aweber.com's Blog Broadcast feature to make all of this happen.

Growing your fan base on social networks like Facebook and Twitter should also be a top priority. Some of your readers will prefer to interact in these venues rather than receive regular e-mails from you. For example, when you use Twitter and Facebook, you can easily promote your newest content to your fans.

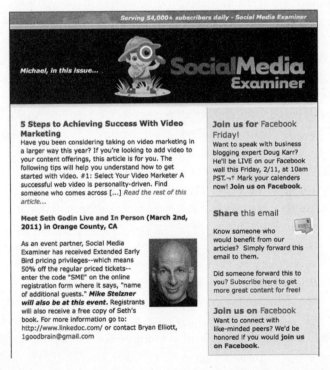

FIGURE 9.3 Here's an example of one of SocialMediaExaminer.com's daily e-mail blasts.

Once you've developed a list of e-mail subscribers, Facebook fans, and Twitter followers, you should regularly feed them links to your free content. The result: You'll have established new channels of communication with your readers. These secondary channels will be your key to future sales growth.

Up to this point I've talked about using marketing messages to generate leads and grow your subscriber base. Is there a way to actually directly market your own products and services?

MARKETING YOUR PRODUCTS AND SERVICES: THE VELOCITY LAUNCH

Once your rocket ship has launched and gained momentum with a sizable subscriber base, you can experiment with promoting your products and services.

It is at this juncture where you need to tread carefully. Marketing is like friction for your rocket ship. Think of it as space brakes. *The more you fire the sales and marketing engines, the slower you'll grow your reader base.* Remember, people are resistant to marketing messages, and they could flee en masse if they don't like what you're doing.

The key to growth is to not overmarket your products and services. Said another way, it's important to know when to flip on and then back off those marketing engines.

Once you've established a strong secondary channel—like the subscriber e-mail list discussed in the prior section—you can begin experimenting with marketing your products and services.

If, however, you're just getting started, you may need to wait a while before you take this step. For example, in the case of SocialMediaExaminer.com, we waited until we reached 10,000 e-mail subscribers before we began activating any of our product promotions. We wanted not only a substantial subscriber base, but also a proven track record in the minds of our readers. It took us about four months to get to this point.

Likewise, Procter & Gamble waited a few months on its property Man of The House before promoting any company products.

If your business is new and you immediately begin promoting it, you'll severely impact the growth of your reader base. And if you can't grow your readers, you'll become a flash in the pan, a one-hit wonder—a "whatever happened to those guys?" phenomenon. Longevity should be your goal.

Here's how to market your products and services.

Over the years I've developed a method for introducing a product, service, or event to people that maximizes sales and minimizes reader objections. I call this activity a *velocity launch.*

A velocity launch is the process of building anticipation and momentum that excites your reader base about your products or services, while also moving them closer to a purchase decision.

A velocity launch involves adding marketing messages to your content and leveraging the secondary channels you've built.

The model typically starts with an announcement via your primary and secondary channels. Momentum is gained by using a carefully timed combination of primary and nuclear content, with a slight promotional bent. The mission of this special fuel is to sell, not to grow an audience.

Like the normal content you regularly produce, this special promotional fuel is also valuable to readers. But unlike normal content, in this content you'll embed subtle marketing messages. Just keep in mind, if you run too much of this promotional fuel through your rocket engines, you'll negatively impact their long-term performance. That's why you should reserve a velocity launch for special circumstances.

Here's an example of how we employ velocity launches at Social-MediaExaminer.com. Our site primarily sells online conferences called Success Summits. These are large virtual conferences focused on topics like social media, Facebook marketing, and blogging. A velocity launch could just as easily be applied to products or services.

For our summits, we typically institute a 60-day promotional cycle, and conduct three events a year. This means that about half the time we're employing velocity launches and the other half we don't promote anything. For our readers, this is a very good balance, and rarely ever raises any "you're marketing too much" objections.

Our promotional-laced content typically makes up a very small percentage of our primary content produced during a launch. For example, we might produce four to six articles over 60 days, relying more heavily on secondary channels and special nuclear content.

We begin by putting together a detailed promotional plan that seamlessly integrates with our regularly produced content. This typically involves video, articles, social media activities, e-mail, and contests.

What follows is an example of some of our common activities during a velocity launch:

Announcement   We begin our campaigns by sending an e-mail to our subscriber base, announcing the event (see Figure 9.4). This e-mail uses the same template and look as our regular daily blasts. Inside the e-mail is usually a very short letter from me, describing the new event and inviting people to check it out.

Webinar   We also invite our readers to an educational webinar. For example, for our Facebook summit, the webinar was titled, "9 Businesses Doing Facebook Right and What You Need to Know" (see Figure 9.5). During the webinar we conducted mini case studies, describing what businesses were doing right. Just before taking questions we made a brief mention of the event.

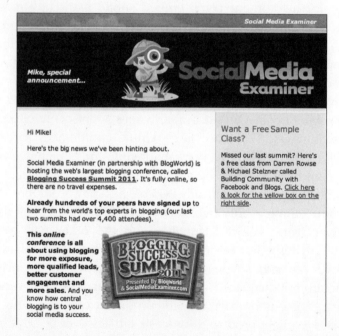

FIGURE 9.4   We sent this e-mail to our subscribers announcing one of our events. Notice the reference to a free sample.

Figure 9.5 Notice how the webinar is formatted in a template showing the logo of the summit we're promoting.

Content-Rich Blog Posts We typically publish three or more articles that are focused on the topics being covered at the event. For example, during our Facebook conference we interviewed presenters and crafted a blog post that revealed tips from the pros (see Figure 9.6). At the end of the post was a brief mention of our event.

Facebook Friday Experts When we have a summit going on, our Facebook Friday experts are summit presenters. This allows us to showcase the experts' knowledge to our Facebook fans and mention that they will be presenting at the event (see Figure 9.7).

Free Ticket Contest We give away free tickets to our events during the peak of our sales cycle. We ask people to write about their most pressing social media challenges and then give two free tickets to our favorite entry (see Figure 9.8). We also randomly draw a winner from

FIGURE 9.6 This blog post revealed tips from our summit presenters.

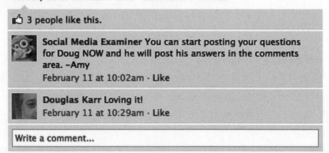

FIGURE 9.7 In this example, Douglas Karr was a presenter for our blogging summit. He answered dozens of questions our fans posted directly on our Facebook wall.

SmartBlog on Social Media

Where SmartBrief on Social Media e-newsletter readers share ideas

| Topics: | Andy's Answers | Emerging Technologies | Events | Ideas in Action | Microblogging | Polls |

Win Tickets to Blogging Success Summit 2011

By Guest Blogger on January 13, 2011 | Comments (85)

UPDATE We have announced our two winners. The winner of the comment/blog portion of the contest, receiving two tickets to the Blogging Success Summit is Felissa Elfenbein, read her comment here. The winner of the Twitter contest is Madonna Kash, a restaurant & food service marketer. Thanks for everyone who participated in the event. We look forward to seeing you all in a couple of weeks!

1,816

Tweet

Share

80

Email

Want to win a free ticket to the largest online blogging event of the year?

Social Media Examiner, BlogWorld and SmartBrief on Social Media have partnered to bring you Blogging Success Summit 2011. And we've come up with a fun way to get you involved.

FIGURE 9.8 Here's an example of a contest we conducted for our blogging summit, in partnership with one of our presenters from SmartBrief.

Source: Reproduced by permission from SmartBlog © January 13, 2011.

among people who tweet about the contest. This generates a lot of buzz and gets people excited.

Newsletter Integration Our daily newsletter contains text-based ads for our summit, and ads for our promotional content (see Figure 9.9). This channel becomes a primary sales channel because people are reminded daily (but for a limited time) about the summit. We update ads to include the number of attendees, familiar brands that will be attending, and reminders of key dates for price increases.

Facebook Integration We add a Facebook event to our fan page, encouraging people to write on our event wall. We also change our avatar to include a graphical ad for our current event. On a regular basis we share our promotional content, remind our Facebook fans to register for the summit, and encourage them to tell us why they're attending (see Figure 9.10).

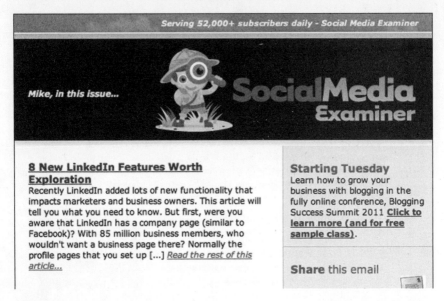

Figure 9.9 Notice how the event is mentioned in the sidebar, along with a free offer.

Internet TV We feature a monthly Internet TV show called *Social Media Examiner TV*, and we make our event the sponsor of the show and have our show host make a brief mention of the event (see Figure 9.11).

Using the velocity launch model we've been able to turn thousands of our readers into paying customers, generating millions of dollars in annual revenue. And we didn't need a big budget. We just carefully crafted special content with a slight promotional bent.

A velocity launch can be applied to many different types of products and services. Whether you're launching new software, an information product, a service offering, or a physical product, a velocity launch is a very effective method.

Let's look now at how a velocity launch might be applied to a product announcement. Let's say the fictional company Customers and Reps Engage (CARE), which has built a strong community of customer service reps, is about to release a new remote diagnostics tool called Reach.

FIGURE 9.10 Here's an example of how we integrate ads into our Facebook avatar.

Here's how a velocity launch might work for this product:

1. CARE decides to produce some nuclear fuel, starting with a survey of its community. The goal is to identify the most challenging customer support issues faced by the industry.
2. CARE then previews key findings of the survey in an exclusive webinar. During the webinar, CARE makes a brief mention of Reach.
3. The leads generated from the webinar are nurtured with additional valuable content. For example, attendees are sent an article with tips on how to deal with angry customers. Those who open the e-mail and click are segmented for a special sales team.

FIGURE 9.11 Here, show host Mari Smith discusses the Facebook Success Summit during one of our Internet TV episodes.

4. The results of CARE's customer service survey are also released in a free report that is actively promoted to its community. CARE's new product is the sponsor of the report. Inside the report is a full-page ad for Reach, offering a free white paper that describes how service reps could improve customer satisfaction.

5. A number of articles are also crafted based on the findings of the report. For example, "Top 10 Customer Service Challenges" and "7 Tips for Better Remote Support from the Pros" are published on CARE's popular Web site. Outside experts are contacted, asking for tips; they are referenced in those articles. Each article points to the free report.

By conducting a velocity launch, CARE is able to achieve a blockbuster launch of its new product.

Although fictitious, it should be clear how a velocity launch can be used to leverage content to fully engage a community. It's the content that gets people excited and opens the door for some marketing.

As the examples here demonstrate, *most of the promotions embedded in a velocity launch revolve around content that contains subtle promotional messages.* This makes it possible both for readers to receive the marketing messages and for companies to sell their products or services.

Note that there's also a strong "other people" component to a velocity launch. Most promotional content—such as webinars, articles, and contests—should involve outside experts in some capacity. When you leverage experts, you'll drive more traffic to your content, while also exposing people to your event, product, or service.

You will begin to experience an increasing velocity of sales as you combine many different tactics together across various channels.

In order for a velocity launch to work long term, however, *you also need to know when to turn off your promotions.* In the case of SocialMediaExaminer.com, this is easy because our products (events) have a clear beginning and end. In your case, this may not be so simple.

You may need to experiment with the right balance of promotional content to see the impact it's having on the growth of your reader base. If you find your business is constantly promoting, you will begin to lose people. I'd suggest you *turn your promotional engines off at least half the time,* or more. This means that you should go at least a month or more between promotions. This should be a time when there is no evidence of any overt marketing messages.

If your promotions have substantially slowed, or stalled the growth of your reader base, you may need to employ some nuclear fuel to get your rocket ship moving again (see Chapter 8). Commercial-free nuclear fuel can quickly flush the marketing messages from your rocket engine.

WHY A VELOCITY LAUNCH WORKS

Using a velocity launch is a powerful way to convey your sales message to people without being overly promotional. It converts the distasteful sales pitch into a palatable promotion. It then takes that promotion and wraps it in a coating of delicious content. *The result is a marketing message that doesn't look, smell, or taste like a marketing message.*

With a velocity launch you make content the center of your promotions. By creating high-value promotional content that occasionally replaces your regular content, you'll be able to sell without offending the masses. Creative articles, webinars, and contests allow your reader base to learn and participate.

After you've built up a large and loyal following, supported by outside experts, you'll find that a small portion of your audience will be happy to purchase your products, services, or events. But *when you employ a velocity launch, you'll greatly increase the chances people will accept your marketing messages and, ultimately, purchase what you have to offer.*

Here are some benefits of a velocity launch:

- *Reduces marketing message rejection* among your readers because marketing is packaged inside of great content.
- *Builds momentum and excitement* among your reader base by releasing a series of content that aligns them to a common theme related to your launch.
- *Enables you to leverage the benefits of nuclear content* while also marketing your products or services.

The reason a velocity launch is so powerful is that it doesn't make the sale the focus. Instead, a velocity launch makes valuable content the core of all activities. Along the way your readers become excited and motivated, resulting in more sales and a growing fan base.

Want to learn more about velocity launches? Visit VelocityLaunch .com for a free step-by-step tutorial on how to conduct a velocity launch.

■ ■ ■

I began this chapter by examining why it's important to cage your marketing messages. I then revealed how to use content to generate leads and grow a subscriber base. Your audience will accept these forms of marketing because they focus on free content.

Finally, I revealed a method to sell your products and services, called the velocity launch. A velocity launch accelerates your sales by making content the center of your marketing initiatives. Unique from normal primary fuel and nuclear fuel, the content used in a velocity launch has a subtle promotional bent, while still containing valuable content for your reader base.

The Last Word: The Elevation Principle Revisited

I know the price of success: dedication, hard work, and an unremitting devotion to the things you want to see happen.
                                           —*Frank Lloyd Wright*

If you want to set your business apart from your industry peers, shift the center of your marketing efforts.

At the core of the elevation principle is great content. It all starts with regularly creating primary fuel to keep your rocket ship moving. This includes how-to articles, expert interviews, and case studies. It's what continues to draw people to your business.

Nuclear fuel gives you the boost you need to quickly attract many people. While harder to produce, the rewards of doing so are massive exposure for your business. Nuclear fuel includes reports based on research, white papers, micro events, and top 10 contests.

Turning to other people is the second part of the elevation principle. This involves finding experts who have access to the types of reader base you want to reach.

You lure experts to you by giving them what they want without expecting anything in return. This often involves helping them promote their books, products, and services. Some experts will turn into fire starters, who can take your business through wormholes to new galaxies.

The final component of the elevation principle calls for restraining your marketing messages. This means only rarely lacing your great content with promotional messages. When content is commercial-free, you'll quickly grow a loyal following that will evangelize you.

When you do employ marketing, focus on promoting your content and growing secondary marketing channels. A velocity launch is a good way to market your products or services on an infrequent basis to your audience. By infusing some of your content with subtle marketing messages, you can effectively guide your readers toward your offerings.

In the end, remember the elevation principle is all about giving gifts. Your great content—freely given without expectation of reciprocity—is a gift that your readers will thank you for. Feed them great content.

It's my strong hope that the concepts I detailed in this book will help you rethink the way you market and grow your business. When content is at the center of your business, your rocket ship will take you to star systems rich with opportunity.

"Do not go where the path may lead, go instead where there is no path and leave a trail," said Ralph Waldo Emerson. There are no road signs when traveling through space. But there is a wide-open galaxy of opportunity.

Where will you go? What will you do?

I look forward to seeing your rocket ship pierce the atmosphere and set course for new destinations beyond your imagination.

Visit ElevationPrinciple.com for some free resources that will help your business succeed, and to let me know how your journey is going.

Appendices

Primary Fuel Content Samples

These appendices contain five examples of primary fuel, as follows (the images were removed to save space):

- Appendix A: Comprehensive How-to Article
- Appendix B: Expert Interview
- Appendix C: Review
- Appendix D: Case Study
- Appendix E: Contrarian Story

How to Use These Appendices
Cross-reference the content you see here with the details outlined in Chapter 7. Study how the articles are composed and think about how you could model them to connect with your ideal reader base.

Comprehensive How-to Article

The following article, by Michael A. Stelzner, was published on December 31, 2008, on Copyblogger.com, just prior to the explosive growth of Twitter.

How to Use Twitter to Grow Your Business

Can Twitter actually help my business, or is it a complete waste of my valuable time? This was the very question I asked myself only a few months back.

Perhaps you've pondered the same?

When people I respect started singing the praises of Twitter, I decided to give it a go. At first I just didn't get it. However, after a short while, I was shocked at the level of access to high-profile individuals I was able to achieve.

This article reveals how bestselling authors and business professionals use Twitter to grow their businesses, and reveals ideas you can employ to achieve Twitter success.

In fact, I used Twitter (and LinkedIn) to source much of what you see here!

First, What Is Twitter Again?

"Twitter is instant messaging made available to the public," stated talk show host and author Hugh Hewitt.

I think that's a fair starting point. I've heard others call Twitter a microblogging platform.

Here's what you need to know: According to the *State of the Twittersphere* report, each day 5,000 to 10,000 new people join Twitter. Current estimates of total users top out around 5 million. That's a lot of opportunity.

Twitter allows you to post updates (called tweets) as often as you want (limited to 140 characters). When you follow other people on Twitter, you see their tweets. When they follow you, they see your tweets.

It's a constant stream of communication. The good news is you can turn it on or off as often as you like. Twitter also keeps a public record of all updates, which can be mined with Twitter Search.

WHY HIGH-PROFILE PEOPLE USE TWITTER

Twitter is not just a fad. When very high-profile folks begin evangelizing Twitter, it's worth closer examination. Here's what some of those gurus told me.

Duct Tape Marketing founder John Jantsch identified three big advantages of Twitter:

> *(1) I get great insight when I ask questions; (2) let's face it, I get traffic; and (3) people on Twitter spread my thoughts to new places.*

Tony Hsieh, CEO of Zappos.com, said:

> *We've found that Twitter has been a great way for us to connect on a more personal level with our employees and customers. We use it to help build our brand, not drive direct sales. It'd be like asking, how does providing a telephone number for customer service translate into new business when they are mostly nonsales-related calls? In the long term, Twitter helps drive repeat customers and word of mouth, but we're not looking to it as a way of driving immediate sales.*

Bestselling author David Meerman Scott said:

> *I have personally connected with hundreds of people I otherwise wouldn't have, and I booked an interview on NPR and a big daily newspaper using Twitter.*

Copyblogger's own Brian Clark said:

Twitter Search is an amazing way to see what people are saying about your products or services. For example, I'll do searches for Thesis Theme and people will be asking questions about our Word-Press Theme. I'll use the reply function to answer the question, which has led to direct sales. Plus, my answer creates awareness of Thesis for others that follow me. It's a form of constructive promotion.

PRACTICAL WAYS TWITTER CAN HELP YOUR BUSINESS

This is where it gets interesting. A lot of people are doing some very innovative things with Twitter. Here are some of their stories.

The Twitter Plan   Cindy King, an international sales specialist, saw a huge boost in business inquiries by implementing a strategic Twitter plan. She explained:

Following the right people on Twitter was key. There are some people very gifted at building relationships on Twitter. As I followed these online community builders, I realized that some of them are also excellent direct response copywriters. They get their Twitter followers to take action.

Lightbulbs went off, and I spent a weekend putting together a tweet marketing plan, and entered in six weeks' worth of tweets, five a day, using TweetLater. I used a mindmap, created categories, varied times on tweets and used BUDurls so I could track results and improve my tweet plan the next time around.

When King finds a spare minute between projects, she logs in to Twitter and watches what folks are talking about. When she tweets, about 90 percent of the time she presents useful information and resources to her followers. The remaining tweets are surveys and questions. Following this strategy, King saw an 800 percent increase in inquiries about her business after she set up her Twitter campaign.

Getting in Front of High-Profile People   B2B copywriter Terri Rylander took a much different approach. At first she was very skeptical of Twitter. "I looked at it but couldn't figure out why people would continually send out messages about the size of a text message, unless they were teenagers. Twitter was for sending updates, they said. I don't have time for updates, and besides, who would care?" said Rylander.

She later came across a peer in her industry who was using Twitter and suggested Rylander follow her on Twitter. "That's when I discovered Twitter as a business tool. I've been in my particular niche for over 10 years and know who the players are (though they don't know me). When I checked who she was following on Twitter, there they all were! It read like a 'Who's Who' list."

Rylander joined Twitter and began following and interacting with the people she respected. "Other than a cold call on the phone or e-mail, I would never have the chance to get my name in front of vendors, industry analysts, and industry experts. I've had a number of Twitter conversations that have also led to personal conversations."

To stay top-of-mind with experts, she offers interesting links, responds to tweets, and posts her thoughts for conversation at least a few times a day.

Getting Traffic and Leads   Pam O'Neil, VP of Marketing at Breaking Point, said:

> *Twitter has all but replaced our PR agency, as a large percentage of our followers are press and analysts. A writer for ZDNet wrote about us and linked to us based on something we tweeted, and that resulted in a huge spike in Web traffic and at least one deal with a major service provider.*

Mike Damphousse of Green Leads said:

> *Twitter is new to us. That said, in a few short weeks we've had a definite increase in all sorts of traffic. Out of the normal inbound leads, the number has increased 15 percent, and two of the inbounds are now active pipeline opportunities. We've found one extremely valuable partner relationship. We are also building PR relationships, although finding the contacts is a bit of a chore.*

Are you beginning to see the potential here?

A Few Tools to Help Your Twitter Experience

Twitter has a whole world of available support applications you can employ to gain the most from the service for your business. Here are a few of my favorites:

TwitterFox: This Firefox Web browser plugin allows you to view tweets within your Web browser (in a popup menu). This is very handy and eliminates the need to constantly go to Twitter.com.

TweetLater: This powerful service allows you to schedule tweets (much like you would schedule e-mails). Another very powerful feature is the ability to receive e-mail digests of keyword activity in the Tweetosphere. This allows you to join a conversation or track topics and trends.

Ping.fm: If you have accounts with many services, such as LinkedIn and Facebook, this amazing site allows you to post updates across *all* of your social media sites in one single step.

Twitter for Facebook: If you are on Facebook, this application forwards your Twitter updates directly to Facebook as status updates.

And just in case you get addicted to Twitter, here's some advice from Chris Brogan, one of the leading authorities on Twitter:

> *Most people who see Twitter the first time either flat-out 'get it,' or they say, 'why bother?' Here's what people miss. They believe one should read every single update that rolls across their screen of choice. Don't. Just let it roll past like a stream.*

So what are you waiting for? Go check out Twitter and report back here with your experience.

Expert Interview

The following interview, by Michael Stelzner, was published on SocialMediaExaminer.com on July 26, 2010.

How to Succeed with Social Media: A Brian Solis Interview

I recently interviewed Brian Solis, author of the new book *Engage: The Complete Guide for Brands and Businesses to Build, Cultivate and Measure Success in the New Web*. He is also co-author of the book *Putting the Public Back in Public Relations*.

During this interview you'll gain great social media insight, discover some key mistakes businesses make, and learn which corporations are excelling with social media.

MIKE: In your book, you made the following statement: "We are forever students of new media. We should never strive to master something that evolves much faster than our ability to grasp its lessons."

Can you elaborate on what you meant?

BRIAN: Yes. We can't rest on our laurels based on the successes of others, because with this medium, *the processes, the techniques, the cultures of social networks are evolving quickly*. So applying templates to them or assuming confidence in past experiences doesn't last long enough for them to be promising for the future.

MIKE: What you're really saying is that you should constantly make sure you are experimenting and studying what others are doing, to ensure that you're on the edge?

BRIAN: Yes, but not just on the edge. You must be able to bring what's on the edge back to the center. In the process, *you actually contribute to the evolution of the industry.*

MIKE: I know you're a big advocate of blogging for business. Can you give us some of the biggest mistakes you see corporate bloggers making, and explain why you think they're making them?

BRIAN: The biggest mistake I see is, they're not blogging. The secondary mistake is that they're using blogs just as extensions of every other push medium they have in operation today, whether that's a marketing sheet or a Web site.

A lot of times I'll read corporate blogs and they're very self-serving, or they're very shallow, or they're just *done* because you're told you need to do it and you're supposed to introduce or inject passion into it.

If you look at 37signals, their blog ultimately became a book in terms of the lessons they share there. It's just a value-added resource. You go there as a destination so that you can learn, and you can walk away with direction and empowerment and inspiration.

MIKE: Let's talk about a big company or two that you feel are doing social media right. What are they doing?

BRIAN: One is Starbucks because they're experimenting. It goes back to the part where we were discussing being a student of new media.

You see what they're doing on Facebook and Twitter. They're absolutely engaging. They're rhythmic. *They have a programming or an editorial calendar in place, and every day there is something new.* There are comments, questions, and polls. There are things that are offered in terms of incentives or rewards.

But they're also doing things that show they're trying to actively grow by going to where people are, specifically. For example, Starbucks did something very interesting with a company called Klout that didn't get much fanfare, but it's really interesting in terms of what's to come in social media.

Klout is a service that allows you to identify influencers on Twitter. Influencers are people who can move the needle around certain topics. Starbucks decided to test it.

[Starbucks] went to Klout to find all of the influencers around coffee, those people who have the ability to drive activity. They went out and rewarded all those influencers with free samples of their Pike's Peak coffee. What better way to reward somebody for their level of influence that they've attained, and maybe earn some relationships in the process, or at least attention?

MIKE: In addition to Starbucks, can you talk about one other well-known company that you think is doing social media well?

BRIAN: Dell. Here's one of the reasons I find them to be so fascinating. This again is a lesson that is taught in my book. There's a whole chapter about this idea.

One of the things that works against any champion of social media is the culture of the company. But really where *the potential of social media is realized is in your ability to learn from engagement and adapt accordingly*, and to introduce or evolve new products and services that are more meaningful to the communities or the marketplaces where you're trying to earn greater market- and mindshare.

Dell has demonstrated that their organizational culture gets it. It's from the bottom up, it's from the outside in, and it's from the top down. Michael Dell believes in this so much that he spends weekends and evenings working with his teams to figure out ways they could be more relevant. Plus, the team gets motivated by it.

One such example that I don't necessarily see or read about is how they attack issues that are basically emerging problems. Dell says, *"Let's monitor for things that are about to go wrong or that are just going wrong now and nip them in the bud."* They pay attention to driver issues or hardware issues as one, two, three, four, or five people start to mention these issues. The minute it hits a certain point, they put a team on it, find a fix, and introduce the solution to the marketplace before it becomes a real problem, before it makes blogs, before it makes the press.

MIKE: What are your views about Facebook fan pages? How important do you think they are today and how important will they be two years from now?

BRIAN: I was speaking at a conference recently and said something that turned out to spark a massive debate afterward. That was, "By this time next year, brands will be spending more time on their Facebook brand pages than they will be on Twitter."

That just sent everybody into a riot. Twitter is beloved. Twitter really puts the "me" in social media, because we bring a little bit of ourselves to that. Even though we do so with Facebook, there is something a little bit special or personal with Twitter.

Twitter has even said this. It's less of a social network than an interest or themed network, where individuals are forming relationships around context or interests.

The Facebook fan page, or the "brand page" as I call it, is a hub that can guide and drive experiences, but also can define them. By "define," I mean it's one thing to have interactions on the wall. It's one thing to respond to comments. It's another thing to be able to customize those tabs.

If you think about it, FBML—that language that you're able to use to customize these tabs—allows you to do some really fascinating things. Not too many people understand that you can actually install Google Analytics on a tab in Facebook so you can start to measure the activity—almost like you can with your Web site analytics, to get intelligence necessary to improve the experiences.

So, *Facebook is probably, in my opinion, one of the most underutilized networks out there,* from a programming standpoint and from an engagement standpoint. I'm bullish on it, if you can't tell.

MIKE: I honestly do believe that's where it's at right now. I actually tweeted recently, "I can't believe I'm actually enjoying Facebook more than Twitter." I almost had to cringe when I said it.

Speaking of Facebook, on our fan page, we posted that I was going to be doing this interview and asked our fans to chime in with their questions. Mari Smith asked, "What is your daily routine and what tools do you use to keep on top of everything?"

BRIAN: I call it the "attention dashboard." Facebook is like an attention hub. I've created an attention dashboard that pulls in content from all different types of sources across multiple networks into one place based on keywords of interest tied to levels of influence, so I can at least get the skinny on certain things.

MIKE: Is this a custom thing, or do you use a public tool?

BRIAN: It's a custom thing.

MIKE: You're going to have to release that as a product.

BRIAN: I released part of it as a product with the help of Christopher Peri. It's a product called FriendFilter. It added this level of intelligence to surfacing the people who are following you on Twitter, for example, but only showing you the ones who might be of interest to you so that you could consider following them back.

MIKE: So the attention dashboard is how you keep up on the hottest and latest trends in the industry, and that's how you decide to write content for your blog? Is that correct?

BRIAN: No, that's how I stay smart. *I write on the things that move me at an emotional or intellectual level, or if there is something incredibly important that I need to share with people,* to get them to move in a particular direction.

MIKE: Where do you see social media headed in the next few years? Give me the mile-high view.

BRIAN: About a year ago, I talked about the idea of syndication and aggregation, meaning that we were going to be subjected to multiple networks to which we'd have to pay attention, as well as mobile networks to which we would also have to pay attention using other devices.

At some point, all of these things are going to have to aggregate in some way, shape, or form, where we could have a strategic presence. Look at services like Check.in, where you can immediately broadcast your presence. Let's say I show up at the Westin Hotel in San Francisco: I would use a service like Check.in to broadcast or syndicate my presence to Foursquare, Gowalla, etc.

Those are all temporary bandages to address a bigger issue. That is, how are you going to manage your strategic presence online? And also, how are you going to stay connected to those who matter to you without having to be across multiple networks at the same time?

What the future holds, I believe, is this idea of semantic intelligence and filtering, which are going to allow a lot of this to work [aggregation and syndication] for you without you having to do everything manually.

We see tastes of this on the horizon even now with companies like my6sense. I don't know if you're familiar with that company. You run your Twitter feed through it; it's able to learn how you interact with the feed. As it learns more about you—and this learning is very rapid—it only feeds you the tweets, or at least at the top-line tweets, it feels would be most appropriate for you, regardless of when they were published, earlier today or at the moment.

It learns, and it gets better as you interact with it. If you follow thousands of people, imagine how wonderful it would work for you over time. Imagine applying that same technology across multiple networks into one stream or into one river of relevance, if you will.

MIKE: Brian, where can folks learn more about you?

BRIAN: They can learn more about me at BrianSolis.com, on Facebook; [on] Twitter which is @BrianSolis; or they can pick up [my] book *Engage*, which is hopefully at a bookstore near them, or definitely on Amazon.com and BarnesandNoble.com.

MIKE: Brian, I just want to thank you very much for taking time out of your day. You've been a great fountain of knowledge. I'm looking forward to seeing some great things from you.

BRIAN: Thanks so much. I do really appreciate it. Congratulations on all your success as well.

Review

The following review, by Ruth M. Shipley*, was published on SocialMediaExaminer.com on February 10, 2010.

The Secrets of YouTube Marketing Revealed

I bet you only use YouTube when your 10-year-old daughter wants you to watch some cute pet videos, right?

But you would never think of using it to market your business.

If I told you that YouTube has a *Science & Technology category, a How-to category, and an Education category*, could you begin to see the possibilities?

Whether you work for a high-tech company, a hardware store, or a university, you might want to learn more about using YouTube to publicize your operation.

Why YouTube Marketing?

Because *YouTube is all about video broadcasting*. And videos are perfect for showing technical equipment, demonstrating a procedure, or giving parents of prospective students a virtual tour of the campus.

---

*Used with permission from Ruth Shipley.

Videos can even show a "talking head" touting the benefits of any product or service. Just like a TV commercial. But you have up to 10 minutes to make your case, not 30 seconds. And it won't cost you hundreds of thousands of dollars.

This is not your father's TV. It's not 97 million Americans watching the Super Bowl on one channel on one day and seeing whatever ads the station selects, whether they want to see them or not.

This is 400 million people worldwide actively seeking information on an estimated 6 million to 9 million YouTube channels every month. Yes, I said *millions of channels.* And watching what *they* want to see.

As of 2009, approximately 100 million Americans watched about 6 billion videos on YouTube each month. Americans performed more than 2.9 billion searches on YouTube every month.

In fact, *YouTube accounted for 79 percent of all U.S. visits to 60 online video sites in 2009.* Google Video was number 2, with a 4.6 percent market share.

What Businesses Can Do on YouTube

Remember, social media is about monitoring and participating in the conversations about companies, products, and services. And finding evangelists and influencers who can help you build your business.

Your customers are already having these conversations on Facebook, Twitter, and YouTube; wouldn't you like to know what they're saying? Wouldn't you like to find those evangelists?

Here are some things businesses can do in a YouTube video, according to the book *YouTube and Video Marketing an Hour a Day,* by Greg Jarboe:

- ◆ Publicize a news event about your company.
- ◆ Introduce a new product or service.
- ◆ Demonstrate a new product or service.
- ◆ Distribute a speech given by the company president, CEO, or VP.
- ◆ Record celebrity endorsements of your product or service.
- ◆ Show conference presentations, exhibits, and speeches.

You can even advertise on YouTube. You can place your own ads on videos that match your criteria. It can be a traditional Google text ad or a video ad to the right of the video player. Or you can place the ad in the lower part of the video itself, as a semitransparent overlay while the video plays.

You can also create a Brand Channel, complete with your logo that gives you many more options than a regular channel. It's expensive, but "YouTube gets a Super Bowl–sized audience month in and month out," according to Jarboe.

Yes, *more than 147 million U.S. Internet users watched an average of 100 videos per viewer in January 2009*. That's a bigger audience than the 97.5 million people who watched the New York Giants beat the New England Patriots in the 2008 Super Bowl!

And it's not just 10-year-old girls. Sixty-two percent of YouTube viewers are 35 and older. Almost half have a college degree, and a similar percentage have incomes of $75,000 or more.

Marketing Will Never Be the Same

Jarboe's book could be used as the textbook for a college-level course in YouTube marketing. He says it will take you eight months to get through it, but don't panic!

The first month will go very quickly because only weeks one and two have any "homework." Basically, just get on YouTube and look around.

Weeks three and four are essentially an outline of the rest of the book. You can probably finish the entire first month in a few hours.

Likewise for week four in the second month. There is no homework; you just have to read one or two pages each day. Piece of cake!

But then it starts getting technical:

- ◆ Month three: You watch top-rated videos so you can learn how to create a "viral" video.
- ◆ Month four: You learn the basics of creating and customizing a YouTube channel.
- ◆ Month five: You learn about engaging with and contributing to the YouTube community.
- ◆ Month six: You learn the principles of digital video production.

- Month seven: You learn about becoming a YouTube partner and advertiser.
- Month eight: Covers YouTube Insight, TubeMogul, and other metrics.

A YouTube channel is the equivalent of a Facebook profile. You create the page and put whatever you want on it. But instead of lots of text, you put lots of videos—videos of all those things that businesses can do on YouTube.

And YouTube allows viewers to rate your videos, favorite them, and share them with friends. They can also upload a video response to your videos, add comments, and subscribe to your channel.

But be forewarned: A TubeMogul study of the viewing of 188,055 YouTube videos found that *half of the viewers stopped watching a video after only 60 seconds.*

Ouch! Do you know what that means?

It means you shouldn't even consider creating a compelling video until you engage the services of an experienced copywriter. A copywriter who can write a video script that grabs your prospects' attention and never lets go.

My only negative comment about this book is the high number of nontechnical errors. Not just misspelled words, but missing words! Of course, your brain will supply the missing words based on context, but I'm sitting here thinking, "Doesn't Sybex have editors?"

Otherwise, this book is a treasure trove of information about YouTube and how you can use it to build your business. In the words of Suzie Reider, head of YouTube advertising, "Marketing has changed, forever—and will change more in the next few years than it has changed in the last 50 years."

Are you jumping on the bandwagon or sitting on the fence?

Social Media Examiner gives this book a five-star rating.

Case Study

The following case study, by Casey Hibbard*, was published on SocialMediaExaminer.com on August 30, 2010.

How Social Media Helped Cisco Shave $100,000+ Off a Product Launch

As early as 2008, networking giant Cisco was well along in its social media evolution. Back then you could find the company on Facebook, Twitter, and YouTube.

Yet something was missing: the hard business case for social media. Like most companies, Cisco knew it was benefiting from social media, but it couldn't prove it.

The launch of a new router using only social media would provide the proof Cisco's marketers were seeking.

The results surprised even the social media enthusiasts. With this single project, the company *shaved six figures off its launch expenses* and set a new precedent for future product launches.

"It was classified as *one of the top five launches in company history*," said LaSandra Brill, senior manager, global social media at Cisco. "It was the crossing the chasm point for us in the adoption

---

*Used with permission from Casey Hibbard.

phase of social media, and helped us *get over the hump of internal acceptance.*"

Cisco Social Media Stats:

- ◆ Web site: www.cisco.com
- ◆ Blogs: 22 external, 475,000 views/quarter
- ◆ Twitter: 108 Cisco feeds with 2 million followers
- ◆ Facebook: 79 groups with 100,000 fans
- ◆ YouTube: 300+ channels, 2,000+ videos, 4 million views
- ◆ Second Life: 150,000 visitors, 50+ events
- ◆ Flickr: 300+ photos, 400,000 views

SOCIAL MEDIA LAUNCH HIGHLIGHTS

- ◆ 9,000 people attended the social media product launch event—90 times more attendees than in the past
- ◆ Saved 42,000 gallons of gas
- ◆ Nearly 3 times as many press articles as with traditional outreach methods
- ◆ More than 1,000 blog posts and 40 million online impressions
- ◆ A Leading Lights award for Best Marketing
- ◆ One-sixth the cost of a traditional launch

Router Launch: Promotion Through Play

Up to that point, the traditional product launch went something like this:

1. Fly in more than 100 executives and press members from 100 countries to headquarters in San Jose, California.
2. Take a few hours of the CEO's or an executive's time to prep and present.
3. Distribute well-crafted—but static—press releases to key media.

4. E-mail customers.

5. Run print ads in major business newspapers and magazines.

For its Aggregated Services Router (ASR) launch, Cisco aimed to execute entirely online leveraging social media, and in doing so, engage network engineers in a more interactive, fun way.

Cisco met its audience where they were—in online venues and the gaming world. Here's how:

SECOND LIFE

The company built a stage with big-screen monitors, chairs for the audience, and palm trees for its flagship launch event—entirely in a Second Life environment. It then piped in video of executives presenting the ASR.

Network engineers or the press could board their own "personal transport device" to surf through a virtual router.

To generate prelaunch buzz, the team held a concert in Second Life, featuring eight bands over seven hours.

An executive presented the new ASR in a live Second Life event.

A 3D GAME

More than 20,000 network engineers learned as they played a 3D game, wherein they "defended the network" using the ASR. (Research shows that 17 to 18 percent of IT professionals play games online every day.) Top scorers went on to a championship round, with the winner bagging $10,000 plus a router.

"If they're playing games, that's how they want to engage and that's who they are," Brill said. "How do we make that applicable to what they do at work?"

YOUTUBE

Additionally, the company heavily used video to educate customers and the media about the ASR, encouraging them to pass along links via social sharing. Video gets eyeballs. Cisco's "Future of Shopping" video went up to 3.3 million views.

VIDEOCONFERENCING

The company's next-generation videoconferencing technology, Cisco TelePresence, brought customers together at local offices around the globe. Executives back in San Jose could see the audience's facial expressions, and vice versa.

MOBILE
A video datasheet engaged engineers on their mobile devices.

FACEBOOK
Hardcore network engineers could connect on the Cisco Support Group for Uber User Internet Addicts. How addicted are they? One member shared that he networked his community swimming pool so he could stay connected poolside.

"It allowed them to connect with Cisco in a new way, and build preference and customer loyalty," Brill said.

SOCIAL MEDIA WIDGET
Cisco assembled videos, collateral, and images in a widget format and embedded it into "social media" news releases and launch pages. Bloggers and others could spread the information easily with the embedded code.

CISCO BLOGS
Videos and other content engaged bloggers and customers, encouraging viral pickups.

ONLINE FORUM
Cisco seeded its Networking Professionals Technology Community Forum with launch-related discussion topics, and gave customers an "Ask the Expert" function.

The whole campaign spanned three months, with the launch in the middle. During prelaunch, launch, and postlaunch, Cisco kept the audience engaged by encouraging discussion with and among its audience.

Reaching 9,000 People
Compared to traditional launches of the past, the ASR launch delivered eye-opening numbers. More than 9,000 people (*90 times more than past launches*) from 128 countries attended virtual launch events. Without travel, the launch saved an estimated 42,000 gallons of gas.

Plus, top executives spent only about an hour recording the video presentation.

Print ads were largely replaced with media coverage, including nearly three times as many press articles as a comparable traditional launch, more than 1,000 blog posts, and 40 million online impressions.

Yet Cisco wasn't the only one recognizing the impact of the campaign. In fact, the company earned a Leading Lights award for Best Marketing.

Taken alone, the reach of the campaign impresses. But consider this: *The whole launch cost one-sixth of a similar launch that used traditional outreach methods.*

Social Media: The New Norm

The ASR launch effectively tore the lid off social media at Cisco, which now truly walks its talk regarding the power of networks. Since then, social networking comes standard with every product launch, and *print advertising funds have largely been moved to social activities.*

And media like video, Facebook, and Twitter keep customers and the press engaged continuously. Cisco now runs live public Q&A sessions showcasing John Chambers, Cisco's chairman and CEO, as he answers questions coming in via Twitter.

Live TelePresence sessions bring executives and customers together for face-to-face virtual meetings.

With subsequent launches, the company has realized even greater ROI—now seeing costs just one-seventh of those before. But the networking company keeps pursuing even greater returns with social networking.

"Now that we've got that buy-in, we need to just continue to show the success of one campaign over another," Brill said.

Tools like Radian6 and Symphony help the core social media team, now eight people, *measure the impact relative to cost of each campaign.* After every campaign, the team just sets new benchmarks to beat.

"Social media doesn't replace the need for white papers or sales interaction. I think it helps *accelerate and shorten the sales cycle,*" Brill said. "There are studies out there that people who are involved in communities and engaged with the brand are likely to spend up to 50 percent more than those who are not. We want to try to prove that."

Four Tips for Success

1. *Listen first.* "For every product launch, our formula starts with listening. We start a list at least a month before of buzzwords and challenges and then figure out the right tools," Brill said.
2. *Use video often.* Web pages with video draw five times more engagement than those without. Cisco encourages video blogging to add transparency to bloggers' voices.
3. *Talk at versus talk with.* Product launches of the past communicated at the audience. Now, nearly all activities have an interactive element.
4. *Always be brand-building.* Not everyone's ready to buy now, especially a six-figure purchase like the ASR. Activities like the online game engaged the loyalty of network engineers, who heavily influence such decisions.

Contrarian Story

The following contrarian story by Michael A. Stelzner was published on MarketingProfs.com on February 24, 2009.

The Dark Side of Twitter: What Businesses Need to Know

Right now Twitter is the talk of the Web among marketers. Use of the elegantly simple social media site has shot into the stratosphere unlike anything in recent memory, and it's businesses that are leaping onto the Twitter bandwagon.

The *New York Times* calls Twitter "one of the fastest-growing phenomena on the Internet." A recent study determined at least 5 million people are using the service, and new members are signing up at a clip of 10,000 per day. And unlike other "here today, gone tomorrow" services, Twitter seems to have staying power.

With companies tightening their ad spending, social media is clearly the next marketing frontier. As with any new craze, there are enormous opportunities and rather large pitfalls that must be avoided.

For this article, I spoke to a number of marketing professionals who've been exploring the Twitter terrain for a while. My quest was to identify the Twitter landmines so you can fast-track your adventure into this vast new frontier. But first, a short story to convey the power of Twitter.

The Shot Seen Around the World

Remember the downed plane floating on the Hudson? How could anyone forget the picture of people crowded on the wing as the plane gently floated in the frigid January river.

Janis Krums was nearby as U.S. Air flight 1549 fell from the sky that day. Just moments after the crash, while onboard an approaching ferry, Janis snapped a picture with his iPhone and posted this on Twitter:

> *There's a plane in the Hudson. I'm on the ferry going to pick up the people. Crazy.*

The few hundred people following Janis began spreading the word to their Twitter followers. Janis couldn't have imagined what was about to happen.

Within 30 minutes he was live on MSNBC and CNN. *Good Morning America* invited him into its studio. Then the BBC, *20/20*, ABC, and *Inside Edition* followed. The morning after the crash, his picture was on the front page of major newspapers across the planet, and his e-mail inbox had more than 4,000 e-mails.

A few days after the shot, he posted this comment on his blog:

> *To say that the last couple of days have been crazy/intense or whatever adjective you want to use is an understatement. It was sheer madness for a while.*

Clearly, Twitter can be a rapid catalyst for good news. And now for the dark side of Twitter . . .

Be Careful What You Say: The FedEx Story

"Everything you tweet is searchable on the Web. This can be good and bad. Good if you're strategically using keywords for which you want to be found, and bad if you aren't mindful that if you're not nice, it can come back to bite you!" says blogging expert Denise Wakeman. And that bite came back hard recently for PR agency Ketchum.

An employee working for the firm landed in Memphis to deliver a presentation to more than 150 people at FedEx. On arrival, he wrote the following on Twitter:

> *True confession, but I'm in one of those towns where I scratch my head and say, "I would die if I had to live here!"*

It just so happened that a FedEx staffer saw the message and forwarded it to numerous company executives. FedEx drafted a response to the Ketchum employee. The last line of the letter says it all: "True confession: Many of my peers and I don't see much relevance between your presentation this morning and the work we do." The story quickly spread across Twitter and the Internet.

This hard lesson is also a wake-up call for many businesses. Twitter is a public communication medium. Everything said is permanently etched in Twitter's digital fabric.

"While Twitter can be effective as a marketing tool, if you are not careful, it can become a viral tool for negative press. Anything typed in Twitter is '*on the record*'," said Steven Talbott, Sr., vice president of Business Development at Caveo Learning & Performance.

Social media consultant Josh Peters suggests, "Treat all your conversations like your grandmother was listening."

"Your company should be clear in its expectations on your employees' Twitter communication," added Kim Kobza, president of Neighborhood America.

Twitter Crack: Yes, It's Addictive

With the slowing economy, people with a little time on their hands are finding Twitter is a great discovery tool—and a great big addiction.

Marketing consultant Rickey Gold explains, "I spent way too much time exploring and tweeting. I was becoming addicted to Twitter and not focusing on what I needed to do. I got behind on client projects; something I never do and something no business owner should ever do!"

"One of the big hurdles when using Twitter is not to let it invade your life," said international marketing expert Cindy King.

MarketingProfs' Ann Handley said, "It is a time-sink. It's easy to get sucked into spending too much time on it, because it definitely has an addictive quality."

Here are some tips to ensure Twitter does not consume you:

- ◆ *Don't read it all.* "You do not have to read every single tweet. Twitter is a stream you dip into for a while, wade around, and then get back on the banks," suggests social media consultant Connie Reece.

- ◆ *Invest regular daily chunks of time.* Many people allocate preplanned blocks of time to tweet and use tools like TweetLater .com to schedule broadcasts that can post automatically throughout the day.
- ◆ *Use Twitter during your nonproductive time.* Ann Handley explains, "I am often on Twitter while reading news, surfing blog posts, answering quick e-mails, or doing other 'short attention' work. I'm also on Twitter in waiting rooms, in traffic, waiting for a lunch date, or when I'm someplace with nothing but my iPhone and time on my hands."
- ◆ *Filter your Twitter traffic.* TweetDeck allows you to set up groups and filter conversations. For example, if you're following hundreds or thousands of people, you can set up filter groups for people such as analysts, publishers, and influencers; and choose to look at their tweets at your leisure.

Trolls and Squatters

There are bad apples in every bunch. Twitter is no exception. Listen to the nightmare faced by Facebook guru Mari Smith.

"I've had a troll stalking me for a while—a wacky guy who 'brandjacked' me with several fake Twitter accounts last summer. He used my avatar and shadowed my every tweet, twisting the words with malicious intent," said Mari.

"At the time this first began, I was horrified. And I tweeted out to everyone that this was some creep attempting to rile me, and that they should block him. But then I quickly realized this only added fuel to the fire—I was giving him the attention he wanted."

Another challenge is folks claiming your name. Believe it or not, there's a rush to reserve major brand names on Twitter. Buzz marketing expert Paul Dunay has identified a list of brands that have been snatched up by squatters looking to sell them to the highest bidder.

If you're not already on Twitter, it might be wise to reserve your name or brand.

Some Tips for Twitter Newbies

For businesses seeking to grow using Twitter, here are a few tips:

◆ "One of the first things you'll notice is that no one on Twitter wants to be 'sold to' or 'marketed to.' They are there to build relationships, and you don't build a relationship by being overly aggressive with your marketing efforts," said Pam O'Neil, VP of Marketing at BreakingPoint.

◆ Cindy King suggests thinking of Twitter like a great big cocktail party. "Twitter friendships are just as limited as acquaintances you meet at a cocktail party. You need to take the conversation to the next level."

◆ "Twitter is about engaging, connecting, and building real relationships. The businesses it works best for are the ones that have a deep understanding of the people they serve," said Internet marketing advisor Jenn Givler.

Glossary

Buyer personas: A clear picture of your target audience, based on their common characteristics, interests, problems, and desires.

Call to action: A suggested activity that guides people toward an outcome.

Case study: Analysis of how other businesses achieved success.

Channel overload syndrome: The experience of being overwhelmed because information is transmitted faster than people can receive it.

Content: Free and valuable material regularly developed to attract people to your business.

Content-focused ads: Marketing messages that drive people to your free content, not your products and services.

Contrarian stories: Articles that examine the opposing viewpoint of commonly held beliefs and practices.

Coopitition: Contraction of "cooperation" and "competition," coopitition describes when competitors cooperate with each other to accomplish a larger goal, even as they compete against one another.

Discovery system: A set of steps regularly performed to ensure you find the best content and people in your industry.

Editorial calendar: A monthly, quarterly, or annual content publishing plan.

Editorial guide: A reference source to help writers create consistently great content.

Elevation principle: The theory that says that to grow your business, you must combine great free content with the support of outside experts, but eliminate overt marketing messages.

Escape velocity: The speed required to ensure your business escapes gravity drag. See also *Gravity drag.*

Expert interviews: The process of gaining knowledge directly from outside experts and then sharing it with your reader base.

Fire starters: Superexperts with raving fan bases who agree to support your business, thereby quickly propelling it to new frontiers.

Genuine gifts: Valuable content or favors you give to your reader base or experts with no expectation of reciprocity. See also *Reciprocity, rule of.*

Gravity drag: The forces that work against the forward movement of your business, including fear, poor planning, or general uncertainty about your mission plan.

How-to articles: Detailed content that explains to your reader base how to solve a problem.

Idea vault: A digital "safe" or database where you can store ideas for easy and quick retrieval as needed.

Markers: Key accomplishments that advance your business toward its goals.

Marketing messages: Overt sales verbiage focused on promoting your business.

Marketing restraint: The practice of withholding marketing messages until your customers are ready to receive them.

Micro events: Free one-hour events that bring an expert live to your audience.

Mission plan: The vision, goals, and set of activities you determine are needed to move your business where you want it to be.

Motion: The collective activities necessary to keep your business in flight.

New stories: Articles that reveal new information, products, or services of interest to your reader base.

Nuclear fuel: Carefully designed content that makes a lasting impact on significant numbers of your readers and experts.

Other people: A group of people who consume your content, along with experts outside of your business.

Outside experts: People outside your company who have access to valuable knowledge that your readers would be interested in.

Primary fuel: Regularly produced free content that meets the needs of your reader base.

Reader base: People who regularly consume your primary fuel—and who may or may not include customers and prospects.

Reciprocity, rule of: The assertion that people are hardwired to respond to a favor or gift by returning one of their own.

Reciprocity marketing: Promotions built around the assumption that others will feel compelled to respond to any favor or gift.

Reports based on surveys: Detailed findings from original research delivered in a free document.

Reviews: Articles that offer an opinion about a book, product, Web site, or service.

Rocket ship: A metaphor for your business as it's fueled by content.

Secondary channels: Alternative communication paths to your reader base, such as e-mail or social media communities.

Social proof: Validation of an action gained by looking to the actions taken by others.

Top 10 contests: Run to identify the 10 highest-ranking people, sites, products, or services in your industry.

Velocity launch: The process of gradually building anticipation and momentum to excite your reader base about your products or services.

Vision statement: A clear written picture of where your business should be heading. See also *Mission plan*.

White papers: Educational documents written to help people solve specific problems in much more detail than an article.

About the Author

Mike Stelzner is a family man who tries to work the principles of his Christian faith into his business practices.

In 2002, the technology bubble burst, hurting his design business. Needing to feed his family, Mike remade himself as a white paper expert. He tinkered with new marketing ideas while writing for big brands, such as Hewlett-Packard, FedEx, Dow Jones, and Microsoft.

In 2006, he released his first book, *Writing White Papers: How to Capture Readers and Keep Them Engaged*. MarketingSherpa later declared him the "grandfather of white papers." He went on to develop an entire industry focused on white paper creation and marketing, and his name became widely associated with the field.

In 2009, he began to wonder whether his marketing methods were transferable to new markets. With very little social media knowledge, he launched SocialMediaExaminer.com, in October of 2009—an online magazine focused on social media.

Within months of the launch, Technorati ranked the site the number-one small business blog in the world. Only 16 months later Mike's site had become one of the top 1,200 in the United States, according to Alexa, boasting 59,000 subscribers and more than 500,000 monthly page views. Since then, SocialMediaExaminer.com has consistently been ranked one of the top two social media blogs in the world.

Within a span of only 8 years, Mike became a dominant player in two very different industries—by using the very techniques he outlines in this book.

Discover More About
the Elevation Principle

The world of content and marketing is constantly evolving. To help you keep up to date, visit the companion site to this book, ElevationPrinciple.com. When you're there, be sure to sign up to receive regular updates from the author and great free content.

Go to ElevationPrinciple.com now and discover more in-depth discussions of the concepts presented in this book.

Index